Fine Wine in Food

Fine Wine in Food

by Patricia Ballard

Edited by Jill Goddard

Published by
THE WINE APPRECIATION GUILD
San Francisco

Published by
The Wine Appreciation Guild
155 Connecticut Street
San Francisco, Ca. 94107
(415) 864-1202
Ca. Toll Free (800) 231-9463   Outside Ca. Toll Free (800) 242-9462

Library of Congress Catalog Number:
ISBN 0-932664-56-3
Printed in The United States of America
Cover Art: Grace Marcus
Illustrations: Jill Goddard
Editor: Jill Goddard
Designed by: Jill Goddard and Ron Kraus

DEDICATION

For Grandma,
who always gave me unconditional love,
and Bonnie and Jerry
who still do.

Table of Contents

Foreword

It seems to me if a recipe called for a tablespoon of herbs, most people would be quite confused as to what herbs to use. The same is true with wine. There is such flavor differences among the grape varietals that to call for white wine or red wine in a recipe is as confusing as calling for those unnamed herbs.

Since we understand that wine is a food, we need to know how best to blend it with other foods to obtain maximum flavors. First, wine adds its own flavor to the dish. Wine also softens strong flavors and pulls out other, more delicate taste. For instance, a soft fruity Pinot Noir would be lost with the flavor of turnips and rutabagas in a winter stew. But a big, peppery Petite Sirah would calm and blend with these foods. The Pinot Noir that would be lost in the stew would make a superb sauce for roasted lamb.

Patricia Ballard has influenced thousands of people through her teaching and writing, to use good wine in food. Her favorite advice and opening statement in all her classes is, "If you don't like a wine well enough to drink it, you must never, never cook with it".

Patricia feels her most important contribution is the research she has conducted over the last fifteen years in matching the most compatible food and wine flavors. This, her newest work, is the result of that research. I hope you enjoy it as much as we have.

Andre Tchelistcheff

In Memory of

Lawrence Bargetto, was my best friend, and as a true friend he became my teacher, my mentor and my greatest source of encouragement in whatever endeavor I undertook.

He taught me the value of time and how to use it. He taught me that mistakes were learning experiences and only became mistakes if you repeated them. He taught me to be careful of my words because once spoken they could never be taken back. He taught me that no living thing was without great value.

He was a thoughtful man with a quick laugh and an eye for beauty. He always knew when you needed his time and he gave generously. Most of all Lawrence Bargetto taught me by his daily example.

Lawrence is gone and I miss him but he isn't dead–he lives in everyone he loved, in every life he touched, in everyone who loved him.

Introduction

Every cookbook should have purpose and intent. My intent in this body of work is to teach you the pleasure of combining fine wine and food with joyous results.

"If you don't like a wine well enough to drink it then you must not cook with it". I wish I had a nickel for every time I've spoken or written these words in the past 20 years or more–I'd probably be rather well off financially. The truth of the matter is people are still cooking with bad, to very bad wines, a fact I will never accept or understand. In general, the people who drink and enjoy fine wines are people who cook with wine. Those same people think nothing of buying cheap, screw cap jug wine for the stew pot and, be still my beating heart, the saucepan. One would expect wine lovers to be the last people to commit this culinary faux pas, but it is common. Let's examine this issue. We know that heat dissipates the alcohol in wine, so what are we left with? Flavor–glorious flavor that intensifies and brings together the marriage of the other ingredients. Precisely the reason we have used wine, rather than water, in the first place.

To take this a step farther, let us pretend you are going to prepare a special dinner for your family and a few guests. Would you deliberately purchase a piece of rancid meat for this meal? Of course not. You are going to buy the very best cut you can find, just as you will look for the freshest and and best quality vegetables available. You will set your table with fresh flowers, your nicest linen and china, and of course, you will serve a fine wine with dinner. Whey then, after all this preparation, would you not use a fine wine to cook the food? Wine is, after all, a food that happens to contain some alcohol.

I can almost hear your moans of anguish–especially from the men who don't cook–over the use of your best wines in cooking. Let me hasten to assure you the results will be well worth your sacrifice. The best way to prove to yourself the value of fine wine in cooking is to prepare one of your favorite recipes using a very good wine instead of the cheap wine you may have used in the past. The results will astound you and do more to convince you of the use of fine wine in food than all my words ever could.

Most recipes call for an average of a cup of wine, some as little as 2 or 3 tablespoons. On the whole, most recipes do not require so much wine that the expense should deter you from the use of the very best. At this point I must confess to a weakness for wine sauces, and they usually consist of 2 to 3 cups of wine. Here I cannot deny the expense involved–only the pleasure of such a sauce–the justification is that we don't make wine sauces every day, just as we don't eat prime rib daily.

Now that we are over the hurdles of using fine wine in our food, the question of what wine to use remains. I often refer to wine as liquid seasoning, therefore it seems sensible to advise you to use the wines you truly enjoy drinking, just as you are likely to use seasoning that are most appealing to your palate. There is an instinct within us to pair white wines with white foods and red wines with red foods. This may be a simplistic approach but not necessarily a bad one if you understand and accept that there are no rules one must follow; only some guidelines to assist you in your quest for the very best flavor. Indeed, what we are after is flavor and since we differ so greatly in our likes and dislikes, it is, to a degree, up to us to do some experimentation on our own. That is what I have done for the better part of my life, with some delightful results. I try not to get hung up on the wine writers hype of nuance and shadings of flavors.

Read a few wine magazines and papers and you may come to the conclusion that this exercise is a happy way of filling up space. I, for one, have never understood what a writer means when he calls a wine flabby: I do not agree that because Chardonnay "A" has a bit of oak and Chardonnay "B" doesn't, my Chardonnay sauce will be ruined by either. It is, after all, a sauce based on the flavor of the Chardonnay grape.

This brings me to an unhappy circumstance within the food and wine industry. In publications devoted entirely to food and wine, one still finds little understanding of the use of wine in food. At the risk of being repetitive, wine adds flavor that is found in no other ingredient. Granted, those flavors vary from one varietal to another, but there is a basic flavor to be found in each varietal that is common to that grape alone. Once you isolate that particular flavor and learn to blend it with other flavors, just as you would with any other seasoning, you will have learned the reason for cooking with fine wine. I may be alone in my belief that the difference between "Brand A" and "Brand B" will change the subtleties of flavor to any great extent. As long as the wine is of fine quality, those flavors will come across loud and clear. If the wine is of poor quality, it adds nothing to the food, as it will add nothing to the meal as a beverage.

I somehow feel that the food and wine industry, of which I am a part, has been lacking in the needed research and development of guidelines for the average person. I am bewildered when I read food magazines that still include "cooking wines" in their vocabulary and down right angry that a respected wine industry newspaper would include a recipe that calls for a cup of Chardonnay or a cup of water! We certainly should be able to come up with better instructions than those. No wonder wine isn't taken seriously in terms of its contribution to great food.

I do not intend this as an indictment of my brethren in the wine industry, but rather a plea to take more seriously that aspect of wine–the preparation of fine food cloaked in the heavenly flavors that the grape alone offers us.

Finally, I am forced into the realization that we live in a fast paced, on the run, processed and shrink pack, wine in boxes society. I don't want my meat and mushrooms encased in cellophane so I can't smell or touch them. I'm tired of advertisers telling me to like premade potato patties and pasta in boxes with artifical sauces. "Chicken Culets" made from God only knows what part of the chicken, if indeed any chicken at all!

Fortunately one can still find little weekend farmers markets where one can purchase beefsteak tomatoes as big a fist, fresh green beans that have a real snap when you break them, incredibly fragrant vine ripened cantaloupes and big fat glistening watermelons. I often find country smoked hams and bacon on the rind and always there are those wonderful brown speckled eggs. Fresh sweet basil perfumes the air and makes one's stomach churn with the need of instant pesto. One leaves such a place with renewed energy; filled with the sights and sounds and the simple pleasures of life–and so I come to the real essence of this work--to share with you the wonderful adventure of exploring that exciting and intriguing world of food and wine.

I wish you and yours love, generosity of spirit and joy in your living,

Patricia Ballard
Aptos, California   1988

About Jill...

When I need goods or services I put the word out in our tasting room and I almost always find what I'm looking for. That is where I found the multi-talented Jill Goddard. I was looking for an artist but got much, much more in Jill. Her philosophy of food and wine parallels mine and we immediately worked well together. She is a born editor with great sensitivity for the work. Jill is also one of my very best testers and her critiques of the recipes have been most helpful to me. Above all, is Jill's skill at anticipating my thoughts and directions and she can work any three people I know right under the table! Her contributions to this work are greatly appreciated.

Antipasto

Antipasto means before the paste (pasta), and was meant to be a time, after work and before the evening meal, in which to relax, sip a glass of wine and enjoy a few bites of food. Antipasto often consisted of such foods as nuts, olives, pickled vegetables, and very thin slices of salami and cheese. Foods eaten casually and with the fingers. This was not meant to be the first course. Today the antipasto hour has become the cocktail hour with everyone milling about, attempting to balance a plate, napkin, silverware and a drink, while trying to say hello to everyone in the room. The food is generally too elaborate and often ends up wasted as it is impossible to eat under these circumstances. The fact of the matter is we have exchanged true entertaining for the loathsome practice of the "cocktail hour".

Brie en Croute

My young friend, Carol, who is the deli manager at my local Nob Hill food store, gave me this recipe and I will always be grateful to her. I use it for every kind of occasion and EVERONE loves it.

Notes from Patti:

This recipe can be as varied as your imagination. You can add just about anything you like from diced chicken to strips of salami. I often sprinkle finely minced garlic along with the basil and a bit of cayenne pepper in top. Change the herbs to what ever is in season–I love to use fresh dill. Don't just serve this as an hors d'oeuvre–it makes a wonderful Sunday brunch served with any good California sparking wine such as Mirrasou Blanc de Noir. It's my favorite food for an after theatre late supper party with a fine Cabernet Sauvignon. This dish may be prepared early in the day and refrigerated until it is needed.

1 large round loaf of extra sourdough bread
2 pie shaped wedges of Brie, cut lengthwise
2 Tbsps. fresh basil, finely minced
2 Tbsps. dry vermouth

Cut top off of bread as evenly as possible. Cut bread into squares leaving about 1" edge and gently pull out the bread from the bottom of the loaf. Set aside.

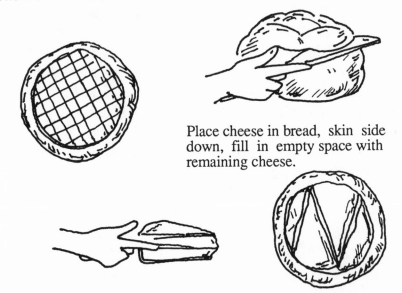

Place cheese in bread, skin side down, fill in empty space with remaining cheese.

Sprinkle with basil and bake in a 375°F oven 15 to 20 minutes or until cheese is completely melted. Sprinkle with vermouth return to oven until cheese is bubbly. Serve with bread cubes to dip into the cheese as you would a fondue. When enough of the cheese is eaten cut the loaf into pieces and serve.

Patti's Salmon Pate

I have made this pate with fresh, frozen and even canned salmon. The fresh salmon is wonderful! The color is a delicate pink, and the flavors of citrus–grapefruit, lemon and orange–from the Gewurztraminer blend perfectly with the richness of the fresh salmon. I was not pleased with the frozen salmon. It tended to be a bit watery. But I was very pleased with the canned salmon. I had not expected to like it. Be sure to remove any visible black skin as you would using fresh salmon. The color is not as pretty, but the flavor is great.

1/2 lb. (2 cubes) butter (only butter will do)
1 lb. fresh salmon, boned, skinned
  and cut into medium size pieces
1/2 lb. fresh mushrooms, sliced
1 large bunch green onions (use half of green tops and
  all of the white root sections), thinly sliced
4 to 6 cloves of garlic, chopped
1 1/2 Tbsps. fresh lemon juice
1/2 tsp. rosemary
1 tsp. dill weed (I like more)
1 Tbsp. dry mustard
2/3 cup Gewurztraminer

Notes from Patti:

I do not like to freeze this pate. It seems to make it smell "fishy". You can decrease the ingredients to half for a smaller amount. I mold this pate in a small fish mold and use sliced pimento stuffed olives for eyes and very thin pieces of lemon peel for scales. It's beautiful!

Melt one cube of butter in large skillet over low heat. Add mushrooms, onions and garlic. Saute for 2 to 3 minutes. Push vegetables to the sides of the skillet. Add salmon and cook until salmon is somewhat white in color. Turn at once. Add lemon juice, rosemary, dill weed and dry mustard. Turn to blend in seasonings. Add Gewurztraminer and cook until wine is reduced to half. Fit food processor with steel blade and add second cube of butter. Add all remaining ingredients and blend until smooth. Refrigerate for several hours before serving. Serves 10 to 12.

Sausage Stuffed Mushrooms

1 lb. medium mushrooms, wiped clean with damp
paper toweling and stems removed.
1/2 lb. sweet Italian sausage, casings removed
1 cup fresh bread crumbs
6 fresh green onions with 1" greens, chopped
2 Tbsps. butter
1/2 cup Cabernet Sauvignon
Salt and pepper to taste

Notes from Patti:

Saute mushroom stems in butter, place in freezer bag and freeze for later use in stews or casseroles.

Fry sausage until well browned and drain on paper toweling. Saute onions and butter until tender. Combine sausage, onions and bread crumbs. Add Cabernet Sauvignon and toss. Season with salt and pepper. Stuff sausage with mixture and place in buttered baking dish. Serve in a preheated 375°F oven for 10 minutes. Serves 10. Petite Sirah may be substituted for the Cabernet Sauvignon.

Zinfandel Meatballs

These tasty little morsels can be prepared early in the day and baked just before serving time.

1 lb. lean ground beef
1 small white onion, finely minced
1 cup Zinfandel
1 cup fresh bread crumbs
1 large egg
1 Tbsp. dry mustard
1 tsp. thyme
1 tsp. salt
1/2 tsp. pepper
12 strips sliced lean bacon, cut in halves crosswise

Preheat oven to 375°F. In a large mixing bowl, combine all ingredients and mix thoroughly, (I use my hands). Form into small balls about the size of walnuts. Wrap strips of bacon around meatballs and secure with toothpicks. Arrange meatballs on baking sheet. Bake 15 minutes turn and bake an additional 15 minutes or until bacon is crisp. Yields 2-3 dozen depending on how large you think a walnut is. Pinot Noir may be substituted for the Zinfandel.

Sherry Cheese Crackers

These are great little do ahead crackers served alone or with guacamole. The dough can be made 3 to 4 days ahead or you can bake and freeze.

1/2 cup butter
1/2 lb. sharp Cheddar cheese, shredded
2 Tbsps. dry sherry
1 tsp. cumin
1/8 tsp. ground red pepper
1 cup all-purpose flour

In a large mixing bowl, cream butter and cheese and sherry and beat until very light. Beat in cumin, salt and red pepper. Gradually beat in flour. Turn out on wax paper and shape into 12" roll. Wrap and refrigerate up to 6 hours. Preheat oven to 375°F. Cut roll crosswise in 1/4" slices. Bake on ungreased cookie sheet 10 to 15 minutes or until edges are browned. Cool on wire racks. Yields 4 dozen. No substitute for dry sherry.

Notes from Patti:

My editor tried to make these in the food processor and it was not a pretty sight! The cheese and butter separated and ruined the consistency–this one needs to be done by hand.

Guacamole

2 large ripe avacados, seeded and peeled
2 tsps. dry sherry
1 small white onion, finely minced
4 cloves garlic, finely minced
1 large tomato, peeled, seeded and coarsely chopped
3 jalapeno peppers, seeded and minced
4 sprigs coriander, finely minced
Salt and freshly ground black pepper to taste

In a small mixing bowl mash avacados with dry sherry. Fold in onions, garlic, peppers, tomato, and coriander. Season with salt and pepper. No substitute for dry sherry. Serves 8-10.

Onions Petite Sirah

My son Patrick is the onion lover of the world. Some of you read about his insatiable quest for the perfect onion dish in my last book. This recipe was one more attempt to come up with yet another way to serve onions. He loves it and so will you!

Notes from Patti:

This is a great "do ahead" dish. It can be made 2 to 3 days ahead and refrigerated. Reheat just before serving. It's also great with meat and poultry.

1/2 cup butter
6 large red onions, diced
6 large shallots, sliced
2 cloves garlic, finely minced
3 Tbsps. sugar
1 cup Petite Sirah
1/4 cup red wine vinegar

In a heavy skillet melt butter and add onions, shallots and garlic. Cook over medium heat for 15 minutes, stirring occasionally. Add sugar and cook, stirring constantly, another minute. Add Petite Sirah and vinegar and continue to cook, stirring occasionally, for another 15 minutes or until liquid is absorbed. Serve on toast or crackers. Makes 3 cups. Cabernet Sauvignon may be substituted for the Petite Sirah.

Roasted Garlic with Toasted Baguette

This is one of my favorite foods, even though it contains no wine. The beauty of this recipe is its adaptability to almost any wine you wish to serve. It is wonderful with a big hearty Petite Sirah but equally at home with a complex Pinot Noir. I have served it at brunch with fine sparkling wine to everyone's delight, and it takes to Chardonnay like a duck takes to water. Try it–you'll love it!

6 large bulbs garlic, roots removed
1 tsp. salt
1 tsp. freshly ground white pepper
1 bay leaf, crumbled
6 leaves fresh sweet basil, finely minced
3/4 cup olive oil (the best you can buy!)
1 baguette

Trim tops off garlic bulbs to expose all cloves. Fit bulbs close together in a small casserole. Sprinkle with salt and pepper. Add bay leaf and basil. Drizzle oil over garlic and tightly cover with foil. Bake in a 325°F oven for 45 minutes. Slice baguette and place on a cookie sheet. Remove garlic to serving tray. Brush baguette slices with remaining oil in casserole. Toast in oven until golden brown. Squeeze out cooked garlic cloves on toast.

Pesto Stuffed Veggies

1 1/2 cup fresh sweet basil
3 to 4 large cloves garlic
1/4 cup best grade olive oil
1 Tbsp. butter
1/4 cup pine nuts
1/2 cup freshly grated Parmesan cheese
2 Tbsp. dry vermouth
20 mushrooms
20 cherry tomatoes
4 carrots
4 large cucumbers
1/2 cup pine nuts, toasted

Place basil and garlic in a blender or food processor fitted with a steel blade. Turn on and slowly add olive oil. Add butter, pine nuts, cheese and dry vermouth and blend until smooth. Set aside. Clean mushrooms and remove stems. Cut off tops of tomatoes and carefully remove pulp with small melon scoop. Peel carrots and cut into 3/4" rounds. Scoop out centers. Cut small ends into match stick pieces. Peel cucumbers and cut into 3/4" pieces, discarding rounded ends. Scoop out centers. Fill centers with pesto mixture, garnish with toasted pine nuts and chill.

Easy Antipasto Tray

1 lb. large mushrooms, thickly sliced
1–16 oz. can artichokes, packed in water, drained,
cut into fourths
1–10 oz. can pitted black olives, drained
1–10 oz. garbanzo beans, drained and minced
1/2 lb. feta cheese, cubed

Marinade

1/2 cup olive oil
1/4 cup white wine vinegar
2 cloves garlic, minced as fine as possible
Salt and pepper to taste
1/2 tsp. dill weed

Cherry tomatoes and parsley sprigs

Mix all ingredients except marinade in a small bowl. Combine marinade ingredients and beat with a wire whisk until well blended. Pour over vegetables and cheese and toss. Refrigerate several hours before serving. Just before serving, arrange on a tray and garnish with cherry tomatoes and sprigs of parsley. Serves 8–10.

Tuna Pate Mousse

Notes from Patti:

This is most attractive in a fish mold. Line a platter with fresh spinach and invert on spinach. Garnish with a slice of pimento stuffed olive for the eyes and slivers of lemon peel for scales. You may also pack this pate in crocks.

2–6 1/2 oz. cans white tuna packed in oil
2 cups fresh bread crumbs
3 large cloves garlic
3 flat anchovies
1 tsp. dried oregano
1/2 tsp. pepper
1/2 cup sweet style Johannisberg Riesling
1/4 cup olive oil
2 Tbsps. lemon juice
1 tsp. red wine vinegar

Drain tuna, reserving 2 tablespoons tuna oil. Fit food processor with steel blade and blend tuna and tuna oil. Add all other ingredients and process until smooth. Pour into a three cup mold and cover with plastic wrap. Refrigerate up to 24 hours before serving. Unmold on a pretty platter. Serves 10. A sweet Gewurztraminer may be substituted for the Johannisberg Riesling.

Bette Mermis Crab Pate

Bette Mermis is an excellent and innovative cook. She is constantly looking for new ideas and as a consequence she has become more creative. Her pate earned her first place in a California cook-off.

2 envelopes unflavored gelatin
3/4 cup dry vermouth
1–10 1/2 ounce can cream of celery soup
1 cup mayonnaise
3 Tbsps. lemon juice
2 tsps. dill weed
1 Tbsp. prepared mustard
1 1/2 pounds crab or 4-6 ounce cans, flaked
3/4 cup celery, finely minced
1/2 cup parsley, finely minced
1/2 cup cucumber, finely diced
1 medium carrot, grated
4 fresh green onions, sliced, white part only
1–6 oz. can water chestnuts, drained and chopped
1/4 cup green bell pepper, finely diced
1–2 3/4 ounce jar pimentos, drained and diced.

Soften gelatin in dry vermouth. In a large saucepan, heat undiluted soup to boiling point. Add gelatin mixture, stirring well. Remove from heat and add remaining ingredients. Blend thoroughly. Lightly oil a 4 cup mold and fill with pate. Cover and refrigerate for 24 hours. Unmold on a bed of lettuce leaves. Garnish with watercress, hard cooked eggs and radish flowers. No substitute for dry vermouth. Serves 10 to 15.

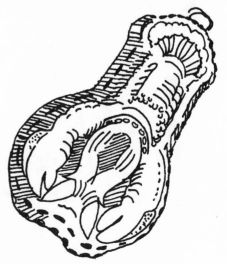

Torta Pesto

This is a feast for the eye as well as the palate and you will receive compliments from all sides when you serve it. The recipe is easy but does take some care in assembling.

1 lb. cream cheese, room temperature
1 lb. butter, room temperature
1 cup pine nuts
1/4 cup dry sherry
4 cups fresh sweet basil, tightly packed
6 to 8 large cloves garlic (I like lots)
1/3 cup olive oil
1 1/2 cup freshly grated Parmesan cheese
A few extra basil leaves

Notes from Patti:

This recipe can be made 2 to 3 days in advance. If you are serving a smaller group, you may cut the recipe in half.

Fit food processor with steel blade. Add half the cream cheese and blend until smooth. Add half of the butter and blend until cream cheese and butter are completely incorporated. Add remaining cream cheese and butter and continue to blend until smooth. Add pine nuts and sherry and blend until pine nuts are broken into small pieces and mixture is smooth. Pour into a bowl and set aside. Clean processor bowl and steel blade. Reassemble and add fresh basil and garlic. Turn on processor and slowly add olive oil through feed tube. Process until smooth. Add cheese and process until smooth. Basil mixture should be quite thick. If not, add a little more Parmesan cheese. Moisten and ring dry a double length of cheesecloth large enough to line bottom and sides of a 7 3/8 x3 5/8 x 2 1/4 inch loaf pan, leaving enough to cover the top of the pan. Be sure there are no wrinkles in the cheesecloth. Make a pretty design with the extra basil leaves in the bottom on the loaf pan. Place a large spoonful of cheese mixture on basil leaves to anchore them in place. Add half of the cheese mixture and smooth carefully to the edges of pan. Spoon in basil mixture a fourth at a time, smoothing carefully to the edges of the pan. Carefully spoon in remaining cheese mixture, smoothing after each addition. Cover the top with cheesecloth and refrigerate 6 to 8 hours. Turn down cheesecloth and invert on your prettiest platter. Gently remove cheesecloth and garnish with more basil leaves or fresh flowers–I once used orchids! Serve with fresh crunchy baguettes. Serves 20 to 25. There is no substitute for dry sherry.

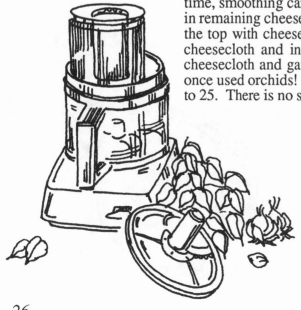

Cold Potato and Leek Loaf

1 1/2 lbs. russet potatoes
2 large leeks, washed and trimmed
1 envelope unflavored gelatin
1/4 cup Sauvignon Blanc
1/2 cup butter, melted
1/3 cup plain yogurt
4 large green onions, sliced with 1/4 of green stems
2 Tbsps. coarsely chopped chives
Salt and pepper to taste

Scrub potatoes and cook in boiling water until easily pierced with a knife point, about 20 to 25 minutes. Drain and cool until potatoes are comfortable to handle. Peel and press through a food mill. Set aside. Trim green stems from leeks. Slice white parts and set aside. Cook stems in small amount of boiling water until pliable, about 10 minutes. Drain and cool. Cut green stems lengthwise on one side. Open stems flat in 1 piece and blot with paper toweling. Generously butter a 7 3/8" x 3 5/8" x 2 1/4" inch loaf pan. Line bottom and sides with stems, leaving enough stems to cover top. Cook white parts of leeks in a small amount of water until tender, about 20 minutes. Drain and chop finely. Stir into potatoes. Sprinkle gelatin over wine in a small saucepan. Let soften for 5 minutes. Stir over low heat until gelatin is dissolved. Add gelatin mixture, butter, yogurt, green onions, chives and salt and pepper. Mix thoroughly. Spoon into prepared loaf pan and carefully cover with remaining leek greens. Cover pan with plastic wrap and refrigerate at least 8 hours before serving. Remove plastic wrap and invert on platter. Slice and serve with CREAMY HERB/VERMOUTH SAUCE. Serves 8 to 10, depending on how thick the loaf is sliced. Fume Blanc may be substituted for the Sauvignon Blanc.

Creamy Herb/Vermouth Sauce

1 1/2 cups heavy cream
4 Tbsps. butter
1/4 cup dry vermouth
1/8 tsp. grated nutmeg
1/8 tsp. cayenne pepper
2 Tbsps. fresh basil, finely minced
1 Tbsp. Italian parsley, finely minced
1 Tbsp. watercress, finely minced
1 tsp. mint, finely minced
1/4 cup freshly grated Parmesan cheese

Combine cream, butter, vermouth, nutmeg and cayenne in a heavy saucepan and simmer, over medium heat, for 15 minutes or until sauce is slightly reduced and thickened. Add herbs and simmer additional 5 minutes. Stir in cheese and serve over pasta or broiled fish. Makes 2 cups sauce, enough for 1 pound fresh pasta. No substitute for dry vermouth.

Escargot Florentine

Escargot is an elegant first course and is even better if prepared up to the baking point, the day before and refrigerated. This allows the snails to absorb the flavor of the garlic butter.

Notes from Patti:

There are special pans for escargot and if you make snails often, as I do, you should invest in them. If you do not have snail pans, use any baking dish lined with crumpled aluminum foil, making depressions to hold each snail shell. I love a crisp, dry, well chilled champagne with escargot. Escargot is always a surprise at a picnic!

1/4 lb. butter (must be butter)
3 large cloves garlic, finely minced (I like lots more!)
3 Tbsps. finely minced fresh parsley
Salt and pepper to taste
2 tsps. dry vermouth
2 Tbsps. finely minced pork fat
24 snail shells
24 canned snails, drained

Cream butter with electric mixer until fluffy. Add garlic, parsley, salt, pepper, dry vermouth and pork fat and beat until well blended. Place 1/4 teaspoon butter mixture into each shell opening, then twist the snail into the shell, small end first. Push snail down into to shell as far as it will go. Cover shell opening with another 1/4 teaspoon butter mixture and place in escargot pans or baking dish. Preheat oven to 450°F. Bake on middle rack of oven for 10 minutes. Serve at once with hot french bread. Serves 4. Dry sherry may be substituted for the dry vermouth.

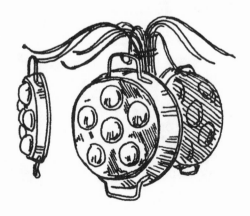

Sauces

"Sauce–by this word is understood in a general way every kind of liquid seasoning for food". This from the epic encyclopedia Larousse Gastronomique. And indeed there are so many sauces from around the world that one could certainly write a book, if not an encyclopedia, about them. My attempt here is to do neither. I only wish to share with you a few simple guidelines I have developed for myself over the years. There is a mystique about sauces in this country that intimidates. But with a good wire whisk, homemade stock and fine wine, you have the makings of some great sauces. I realized stocks are not usually grouped with sauces but since I wish to emphasize their importance, I have chosen to include them in this chapter. I cannot over emphasize the importance of homemade sauces and other aspects of everyday cooking. Homemade stocks are not hard to make! They are not even that time consuming, but you do have to keep an eye on them. I like to keep beef bones and chickens (purchased on sale) in my freezer for those days devoted to laying around the house when I suddenly decide to make stock. I know some of you may think sure, what else does she do in her spare time...but once you actually make stock and find what magic it will perform for you, then you will know I do not speak with forked tongue.

A sauteed chicken breast may be very good, but a sauteed chicken breast topped with a sauce of Chardonnay and cream becomes a feast for the palate and eye. One considers a perfect strawberry inviting, yes, but that same strawberry dipped in a rich, creamy chocolate sauce becomes irresistible.

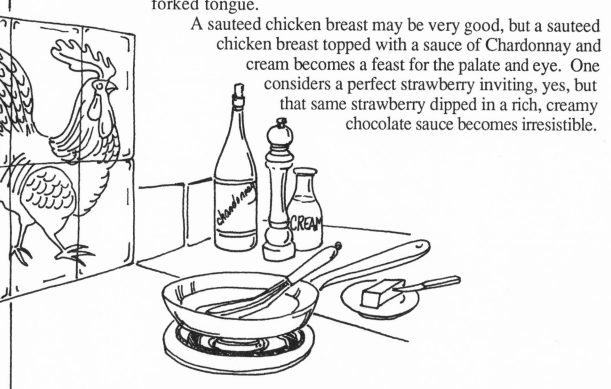

Patti's Pesto Butter

I could not be without this butter in our house. We use it for everything–not just pasta. My sons love it on toasted English muffins for breakfast. Great on baked potatoes and steamed vegetables and a great flavor treat in omelets.

4 cups fresh sweet basil
3 Tbsps. olive oil
1 HEAD of garlic, separated and peeled
1 lb. butter (must be butter), room temperature
1 1/2 cups pine nuts
1 cup freshly grated Parmesan cheese

Place fresh basil in a food processor fitted with a steel blade. Turn on and add oil in steady stream through feed tube. Add half of the garlic and butter and process until smooth. Add remaining garlic and butter and continue to blend. Add pine nuts and cheese and blend until smooth. This butter refrigerates well for up to three months, but it will never last that long!

A Different Pesto Sauce

I love garlic and pesto but when a customer at the winery gave me this recipe I was a real "Doubting Thomas". I was, however, intrigued by the use of wine and this has become my favorite pesto.

1 1/2 cups fresh basil
1/2 cup parsley
14 (this is not a misprint!) cloves of garlic
1 cup olive oil
1/2 cup Johannisberg Riesling, sweet style
1/4 cup pine nuts
Pinch of salt

Place basil, parsley and garlic in a food processor fitted with a steel blade. Turn on processor and add olive oil in a steady stream through feed tube. Add Johannisberg Riesling, pine nuts and salt and process until smooth. Makes 1 1/2 cups pesto.

Aioli

Among the most famous sauces of the world, this golden garlic mayonnaise is wonderful with vegetables, fish and meats.

4 large cloves garlic (I use 6)
2 large egg yolks
1 tsp. dry mustard
1/4 tsp. salt
1/4 tsp. white pepper
1 cup olive oil
1 1/2 Tbsps. lemon juice

Have all ingredients at room temperature. Combine garlic, egg yolks, mustard, salt and pepper in the bowl of a food processor fitted with a steel blade. Process until smooth. With motor running, remove plunger from feed tube and slowly pour in half the oil in a slow steady stream. Stop the motor and scrape down sides of bowl. Turn on motor and slowly add lemon juice, then remaining oil, again in a slow steady stream. Process until sauce thickens. Chill. Makes 1 1/2 cups.

Aunt Mary's Garlic Mustard

When my Great Aunt Mary made her special garlic mustard, it was time consuming because she had to break up the seeds with a rolling pin. Today I just throw everything into my food processor and it's finished in seconds.

1/4 cup mustard seeds
1/4 cup red wine vinegar
1/4 cup Barbera
1/4 cup water
1/4 tsp. ground allspice
1/2 tsp. honey
6-7 grinds of black pepper
2 large cloves garlic, finely minced (I like more)
1 tsp. salt
1 bay leaf, finely crumbled

Combine mustard seeds, wine vinegar and Barbera in a non-metal bowl and let stand at room temperature, for 4 to 5 hours. Pour mixture into bowl of food processor fitted with a steel blade. Add remaining ingredients and process until smooth. Pour mixture into the top of a double boiler. Stir over simmering water 6 to 8 minutes until mustard has thickened. Pour into crock or jar and cool to room temperature. Cover and refrigerate. Makes about 1 cup. Petite Sirah may be substituted for Barbera.

Notes from Patti:

This delicious sauce will keep nicely up to 10 days. Add tiny cooked shrimp to the sauce and spoon it into the center of a cooked "dechoked" artichoke — a great luncheon dish.

Notes from Patti:

This hearty mustard keeps indefinitely and is a wonderful accompaniment to cold meats of every kind. If you like a little crunch to your mustard, process carefully so the mustard seeds are just broken into pieces.

Wine Butter Sauce

This simple sauce is often called Beure Blanc on restaurant menus.

Notes from Patti:

This is my favorite sauce for fish. Spread 2 table-spoons on each plate and top with fish, garnish with lemon and parsley.

3 Tbsps. white wine vinegar
3 Tbsps. Chardonnay
2 small shallots, minced
2 sticks well chilled unsalted butter,
*   cut into 16 tablespoons*
Salt and freshly ground white pepper

Boil vinegar, wine and shallots in a small heavy saucepan until mixture is reduced to 1 tablespoon. Remove from heat and whisk in 2 tablespoons butter. Place over low heat and whisk in remaining butter, 1 tablespoon at a time, completely incorporating each piece before adding next. If sauce breaks down at any time, remove from heat and whisk in cold piece of butter. Season with salt and pepper. Makes 1 cup. White Burgundy may be substituted for Chardonnay.

Mulled Zinfandel Sauce

This sauce is wonderful served over ice cream or poached fruit such as pears. Simply sinful over baked apples!

Notes from Patti:

This is basically a dessert sauce, but I often alter it for pork, venison and wild birds, such as pheasant or duck. Just cut the sugar in half and use a big bodied Petite Sirah or Barbera in place of Zinfandel.

2 cups Zinfandel
1/2 cup sugar
1 cinnamon stick, 2 inches long
2 whole allspice
2 whole cloves
1 inch strip lemon zest
1 inch strip orange zest
2 tsps. cornstarch, dissolved in 2 tablespoons water
1 Tbsp. current jelly

In a 1 quart saucepan, bring Zinfandel, sugar, cinnamon, allspice, cloves, lemon and orange zest to a boil and continue to cook, stirring constantly, until sugar is dissolved. Lower heat and simmer until mixture is reduced to about 1 cup. Remove from heat, strain mixture and return to pan. Set over low heat and stir in cornstarch mixture. Cook, stirring constantly until thick and bubbly. Remove from heat and stir in jelly until melted and smooth. Cool to room temperature. Makes 1 cup.

Great Aunt Mary's Onion Sauce

This sauce has been in our family for as long as I can remember. Aunt Mary always served it with pork roast and I love it with roasted chicken.

2 Tbsps. butter
2 large white onions, coarsely chopped
4 large cloves garlic, finely minced
2 Tbsps. tomato paste
2 Tbsps. sweet vermouth
1 Tbsp. red wine vinegar
Salt and freshly ground black pepper to taste

Melt butter in a large heavy skillet. Add onions and garlic and saute until onions are golden. Add tomato paste, vermouth and vinegar. Add salt and pepper and stir. Reduce heat to low and simmer for about 20 minutes or until thick. Serves 6. Cream sherry may be substituted for the sweet vermouth.

Notes from Patti:

This sauce can be made early in the day and re-heated just before serving.

Phyllis Larsen's Plum Blossom Sauce

Phyllis is a friend who has been with Ghiradelli Chocolate for many years, and no stranger to recipe development. I am flattered she developed this recipe especially for this book. Thanks Phyllis!

1–1 lb. can purple plums in heavy syrup
3 pieces candied ginger
1 dried red chili pepper
1/2 cup plum wine
1 tsp. sugar (optional)
1–2 drops red coloring

Remove pits from plums, reserving syrup. Chop ginger finely. Remove seeds from chili peppers; cut up skin and soak in small amount of hot water (use 1/2 pepper if a less hot sauce is desired). Combine all ingredients in blender and blend until smooth. In heavy saucepan or in microwave oven, heat blended sauce to boiling. Simmer, uncovered, for 30-40 minutes or until sauce is very thick. The sauce may be prepared in advance and kept refrigerated until ready to use. Makes 1 1/3 cups sauce. Delicious served over baked chicken, pork chops or crispy roast duck. For a decorative touch, serve each plate with a colorful fresh flower blossom from your garden. After taking many fun oriental cooking classes, I developed this favorite recipe for American taste.

Patti's Fast Mustard / Chardonnay Sauce

Notes from Patti:

This is one of those wonderful little recipes that goes with so many foods. It's wonderful with cold breaded chicken cutlets. Add some finely minced garlic and serve it with hot or cold rare roast beef. Our winemaker, Paul Wafford, adds a little lemon juice and serves it with broiled salmon steaks.

1/2 pint sour cream
3 heaping Tbsps. mayonnaise
2 Tbsps. Chardonnay
2 Tbsps. Dijon style mustard
1 tsp. lemon zest, finely minced
1/2 tsp. dill weed (I like more)

Place sour cream and mayonnaise in a bowl and blend with wire whisk. Add Chardonnay, mustard, lemon zest and dill weed and whisk until smooth.

Mustard Sauce

1 cup mayonnaise
3/4 cup Dijon style mustard
1 large clove garlic, minced
1 tsp. Worchestershire sauce

Place all ingredients in a blender or food processor fitted with a steel blade and blend until smooth. This sauce is great with pork, fresh asparagus and pan fried fish.

Red Bell Pepper Sauce

I love the look of this sauce. It's delicious over pasta of course but try it with a rack of lamb or drizzled over asparagus.

4 medium red bell peppers
1 medium onion, coarsely chopped
2 shallots, coarsely chopped
1 Tbsp. butter
1/2 cup Sauvignon Blanc
3/4 cup cream
3/4 cup creme fraiche
Salt to taste
4 Tbsps. COLD butter

Spear a bell pepper on a long-handled fork and hold over an open flame until skin is blistered and charred all over. Place in a plastic bag and seal. Repeat with remaining peppers. Set peppers aside for 10 minutes. Remove peppers from bags, peel, seed and coarsely chop. Saute onions, shallots, and peppers in a large saucepan in 1 tablespoon butter until onions are transparent. Add win, raise heat, and cook until liquid is reduced to not more than 1 teaspoon. Add cream and creme fraiche. Continue to cook until reduced to a sauce-like consistency. Pour into a food processor or a blender and puree. Strain and return to saucepan. Add salt if needed. Just before serving, bring to a boil, reduce heat to low and whisk in butter a little at a time until all the butter is incorporated.

Cream Fraiche

1 cup heavy cream
1 cup dairy sour cream

Whisk heavy cream and sour cream together until well blended. Cover loosely with a kitchen towel and let stand in a reasonably warm spot overnight, or until thickened. Remove towel, cover with plastic wrap and refrigerate for 6 to 8 hours.

Notes from Patti:

I am almost never without this wonderful culture. It can be boiled without fear of separation and adds a zesty flavor and wonderful body to sauce. I use it over fresh fruit and vegetables. Cream Fraiche will keep up to 2 weeks.

Chicken Stock

Notes from Patti:

If using a whole chicken, remove skin and bones and discard. Divide meat into 3 equal amount and freeze for future use. A favorite way to use some of the fresh stock is to brown a cup of long grain rice in a large skillet and add 2 cups fresh stock, along with a chopped onion, some sweet peppers, some chicken from the stock, etc. When the rice has absorbed the stock, add whatever else you may have, such as a zucchini or some broccoli and steam until the vegetables are fork-tender.

Stocks are good for only 3 to 4 days refrigerated, so plan to freeze at least half of the stock. For me, half pint and pint containers are most convenient.

1–4 to 5 lb chicken with giblets, or the equivalent in
 necks and backs with 3 or 4 gizzards
1 large onion, peeled and stuck with 2 cloves
2 large carrots, peeled and cut in half
3 large cloves garlic, peeled and cut in half
3 ribs celery, with leaves, cut in half
1 bay leaf
1 tsp. dried thyme
6 peppercorns

Place chicken in a large pot and cover with warm water. Bring to boil. Boil for three minutes, drain and rinse. Transfer chicken to a large pot. Add remaining ingredients and cover with 6 quarts of cold water. Bring to a boil and boil for 5 minutes. Skim off the scum with a large spoon or wire skimmer. Continue to boil and skim for another 5 minutes. Reduce heat, partially cover and simmer for 2 to 2 1/2 hours. If using a whole chicken, carefully remove to a platter and set aside to cool. If using necks and backs, strain the stock through a sieve into a large pot, discarding chicken parts and vegetables. Cool to room temperature. When cool enough to easily handle, line a sieve with a double layer of cheesecloth and strain again. Refrigerate stock until cold. Carefully remove the layer of fat that has solidified on top. Yields 2 1/2 to 3 quarts stock.

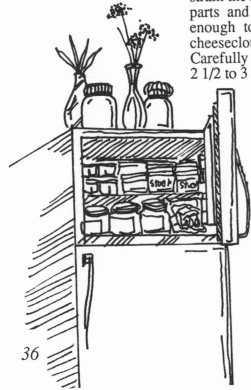

Beef Stock

4 lbs. meaty beef bones, such as neck bones and shanks
1 veal knuckle, cracked
1/4 cup corn oil
2 large yellow onions, coarsely chopped
4 large cloves garlic, peeled and cut in half
3 large carrots, peeled and cut in thirds
2 small parsnips, peeled and coarsely chopped
2 bay leaves
4 cloves
12 peppercorns
1–6 oz. can tomato paste

Preheat oven to 400°F. Spread bones and veal knuckle in a single layer in shallow baking pan. (If you don't have a pan large enough use 2 small pans). Bake 45 minutes. Turn bones and drain rendered fat. Return to oven and bake another 45 minutes or until bones are very brown. Heat oil in a 6 to 8 quart pot. Add onions, garlic, carrots and parsnips and cook until well browned, about 20 to 25 minutes. Remove bones from oven and drain off any remaining fat. Add browned bones and veal knuckle, bay leaves, cloves, peppercorns and tomato paste. Blot up any remaining fat with paper toweling from roasting pan and set over high heat. Bring to a boil, scraping up any particles from the bottom and sides of pan. Pour liquid into pot and add 5 to 6 quarts of water or enough to cover ingredients well. Set pot over medium heat and slowly bring to a boil. Skim off the scum with a large spoon or wire skimmer. Reduce heat and simmer, partially covered for 4 hours. Strain the stock through a sieve into a large pot, discarding bones and vegetables. Cool to room temperature. When cool enough to easily handle, line a sieve with a double layer of cheesecloth and strain again. Refrigerate stock until cold. Carefully remove the layer of fat that has solidified. Yields 2 to 2 1/2 quarts stock.

Champagne Sauce for Fish

3/4 cup Champagne
1 shallot finely chopped
3/4 cup clam juice or fish stock
1/2 cup cream
2 Tbsps. soft butter
1 Tbsp. flour
Pepper to taste

In a heavy saucepan, rapidly boil champagne and shallots for 2 minutes. Add clam juice and continue to reduce liquid to 3/4 cup. Add cream and bring to boil. Mix butter and flour into paste. Lower heat and whisk in butter and flour mixture a little at a time.

Dilled Cucumber Sauce

1 large cucumber, peeled, seeded and diced
1 cup sour cream
1/2 tsp. dill weed
1/4 tsp. white pepper
2 large fresh green onions finely chopped
  with part of greens
1 tsp. minced parsley
1 1/2 Tbsps. fresh lemon juice

Combine all ingredients and whisk thoroughly. Chill at least 1 hour before serving. Makes 2 cups.

Artichoke Cream Sauce

This sauce is so good with spinach pasta and I often use it for cold pasta salads with lots of vegetables.

1–14 ounce can artichokes, packed in water, drained
1 1/2 cups plain yogurt
2 Tbsps. lemon juice
1 small clove garlic, minced as fine as possible
2 Tbsps. freshly grated Parmesan cheese
1 tsp. basil
2 Tbsps. fresh chopped parsley

Place all ingredients in a food processor fitted with a steel blade. Blend until smooth. Makes 3 cups.

Notes from Patti:

Today you can buy spinach, beet and carrot flour at most houseware stores to be added to all-purpose flour. The flavor and color is superb and it is so simple to use.

Salads

Salads are often relegated to a place of unimportance in the scheme of dining. We eat them without attention to their appearance or taste, as a sort of stopgap to our appetites! Perhaps our custom of serving the salad before the main course has contributed to this inattention. In fact, salads are not restricted to wedges of iceburg lettuce, smothered with a thick, sweet, off–orange colored bottled dressing. They can be a meal unto themselves, as is the elegant salade nicoise. The list of ingredients range from pasta to fresh fruits and anything in between your imagination allows. It's time to leave browned wilted lettuce and canned fruit cocktail dotted with tiny marshmallows to others.

Orange Avocado Salad

3/4 cup olive oil
1/4 cup orange juice
3 Tbsps. red wine vinegar
2 Tbsps. honey
1/2 tsp. poppy seeds
1/2 tsp. dry mustard
1/2 tsp. celery seeds

In a jar with a tight fitting lid, combine all ingredients and shake well. Refrigerate.

2 large navel oranges, peeled, white pith
*   removed and sliced in 1/4" slices*
2 large avocados, halved, pitted, peeled and
*   sliced 1/4" thick*
1 large red onion, peeled and sliced into 1/4"
*   slices*
Green leaf lettuce leaves
6 pitted black olives, sliced

Arrange orange, avocado and onion slices around outer edge of a round platter. Tear lettuce leaves and place in center of platter. Top with more orange slices. Sprinkle with olives. Shake dressing and pour over salad. Serves 6.

Zucchini Salad

When you have cooked zucchini 101 ways and you can't face one more zucchini, this is a refreshing, different way to serve this prolific vegetable.

4 to 5 small zucchini, ends removed and sliced into
    1/4" rounds
2 fresh green onions, white parts only, sliced
1/3 cup olive oil
1/3 cup white wine vinegar
1/4 cup sweet relish
1 large clove garlic, minced
3 Tbsps. pimentos, chopped
Salt and freshly ground black pepper to taste

Combine zucchini and green onions in a salad bowl. Combine remaining ingredients in a small bowl and whisk until well blended. Pour over zucchini and onions and toss. Cover with plastic wrap and refrigerate several hours before serving. Serves 4.

My Favorite Summer Salad

This is a gorgeous looking salad that will make your mouth water.

8 bibb lettuce leaves
3 large ripe beefsteak tomatoes, sliced 1/4" thick
2 large cloves garlic, finely minced
12 medium size fresh sweet basil leaves, torn in small
  pieces
2 Tbsps. white wine vinegar
1/4 cup olive oil
1/2 cup crumbled feta cheese

Line a platter with lettuce leaves. Overlap tomato slices, making 3 rows. Sprinkle garlic evenly over tomatoes. Sprinkle basil over and around tomatoes. Sprinkle with vinegar and drizzle with oil. Sprinkle cheese overall. Cover with plastic wrap and refrigerate several hours before serving.

Notes from Patti:

You can add just about anything to this salad from fresh sliced green onions, sliced hard cooked eggs, drained capers or drained anchovies. I always make this salad in the morning giving the flavors time to "marry" and intensify.

Rice Salad

2 cups raw rice
3 cups chicken stock (preferably homemade)
1 large bell pepper, seeded and diced
3 ribs celery, diced
6 to 8 fresh green onions, sliced with half of green stems
1/2 cup minced parsley
1 cup sliced pimento stuffed olives
3–6 ounce jars marinated artichokes, drained, diced, and
  marinade reserved

Dressing #1
1 cup mayonnaise
1 tsp. curry powder
Marinade from 1 jar of artichokes

Dressing #2
3/4 cup good virgin olive oil
3 large cloves garlic, finely minced
3-4 Tbsps. red wine vinegar
1/2 tsp. dill weed

Cook rice in chicken stock until tender. Cool to room temperature. Add remaining salad ingredients and toss thoroughly with either dressing.

Marinated Green Bean Salad

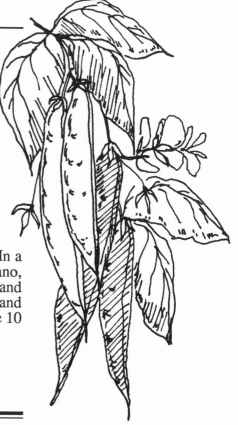

1 lb. fresh green beans, ends trimmed and
  strings removed
1/4 cup white wine vinegar
1/4 cup olive oil
2 cloves garlic, finely minced
1/2 tsp. salt
2 Tbsps. grated onion
1/4 tsp. thyme, crushed
1/4 tsp. oregano, crushed
1/2 lb. mushrooms, thickly sliced
2 Tbsps. pimento, finely chopped

Steam green beans until tender-crisp, drain and set aside. In a large saucepan, combine vinegar, oil, garlic, salt, onion, oregano, and thyme and bring to a simmer. Add mushrooms, cover and simmer, 8 to 10 minutes. Remove from heat, add green beans and mix thoroughly. Pour into a container with a lid and refrigerate 10 to 12 hours. Stir in pimento just before serving. Serves 6.

Dilled Carrot Salad

2 lbs. small carrots, pared and trimmed
1/2 cup olive oil
1/2 cup white wine vinegar
1/8 tsp. white pepper
2 Tbsps. cream sherry
Curly endive lettuce leaves
2 Tbsps. fresh dill, chopped

Notes from Patti:

If you would like to dress up this delicious salad, divide the carrots into six bunches and tie each bunch with strips of pimento.

Drop carrots into boiling salted water and cook until tender-crisp, 4 to 5 minutes. Drain in a colander and cool under cold running water. Pat dry and cut into julienne strips. Mix together olive oil, vinegar, pepper and cream sherry. Pour over carrots and mix thoroughly and refrigerate several hours. Just before serving, arrange lettuce leaves on salad plates. Add carrots and sprinkle with dill weed. Serves 6. Sweet vermouth may be substituted for cream sherry.

Cold Pasta and Vegetable Salad

You can make a meal of this dish first by adding drained tuna and lots of salami cut in strips. Serve with crusty sourdough bread and a good bottle of Cabernet Sauvignon.

Notes from Patti:

Cold pasta salads are as old as Italy and as varied as her people. You can use any style of the thicker pastas that will hold up to a marinade. As for vegetables, use whatever combination you like.

6 qts. boiling salted water
1 lb. farfalloni (big bows)
2 Tbsps. olive oil
2 large carrots, peeled and sliced on the slant
1 bunch broccoli, cut into flowerettes
1/2 lb. snow peas, ends and strings removed
1 lb. fresh mushrooms, sliced
1–1 lb. can pitted black olives, drained
1–1 lb. can pitted green olives, drained
2–6 oz. jars marinated artichoke hearts, drained and cut into fourths
3/4 cup olive oil
1/2 cup red wine vinegar
5 large cloves garlic, finely minced
1 tsp. dried rosemary
1 tsp. dry mustard
1/2 tsp. dill weed
Salt and freshly ground pepper to taste

Add pasta to boiling salted water and cook 5 to 6 minutes until tender but firm. Drain and pour into a large bowl. Toss with 2 tablespoons oil and set aside. Steam carrots tender-crisp and set aside. Steam broccoli tender-crisp and set aside. In a jar with a tight fitting lid, combine oil, vinegar, garlic, dry mustard, rosemary and dill. Cover and thoroughly shake. In a large bowl combine carrots, broccoli, snow peas, mushrooms, olives and artichoke hearts. Toss, add pasta and toss again. Shake dressing again and pour over salad. Toss until all ingredients are coated with dressing.

Ricciolini Salad

Ricciolini means little curls, or, as we know it, spirals of pasta.

6 qts. boiling salted water
1/2 lb. spinach ricciolini
1/2 lb. egg ricciolini
4 green onions with 2" of green stems, sliced
1/2 green bell pepper, stem seeds and ribs removed,
*   coarsely chopped*
12 pitted black olives, sliced
3/4 cup olive oil
1/3 cup red wine vinegar
2 large cloves garlic, minced
1 Tbsp. dry mustard
1 tsp. dill weed
Salt and coarsely ground black pepper to taste

Add pasta (spinach and egg) to boiling salted water. Cook 5 to 6 minutes or until tender but firm. Drain and set aside. In a jar with a tight fitting lid, combine oil, vinegar, garlic, mustard and dill. Cover and thoroughly shake. Combine pasta with onions, peppers and olives and toss. Add dressing and toss. Season with salt and pepper and toss again. Chill. Serves 6.

Notes from Patti:

You can double or even triple this recipe. Great for buffet tables and picnics alike. Surprise someone you love by tucking a container of this salad in their brown bag lunch.

Spinach Mussel Salad

This is one of my family's favorite dishes and I always have a host of volunteers during the season (November-April) to gather mussels for me.

1lb. fresh spinach, washed with stems removed
2 Tbsps. white wine vinegar
salt and freshly ground pepper to taste
2 lbs. mussels, cleaned and debearded
1/2 cup French Colombard
2 Tbsps. olive oil
2 Tbsps. butter
1 1/2 tsp. ginger, chopped
3 large cloves garlic, chopped (I like a lot more!)

Dry the spinach leaves and toss in a large salad bowl with wine vinegar and salt and pepper. Set aside. Steam the mussels in a heavy saucepan with a tight lid, in the wine 4 to 5 minutes. Remove and shuck. Heat oil and butter in a heavy skillet. Add mussels, ginger and garlic. Saute quickly, not more than 2 to 3 minutes. Pour over spinach and serve on warm plates. Serves 4. Fume Blanc may be substituted for the French Colombard.

Winey Mushrooms

These mushrooms take on a faintly pink tinge from the White Zinfandel that makes them especially appealing when served as a salad.

2 cups White Zinfandel
3/4 cup olive oil
4 fresh green onions with 1" of green stems, sliced
Zest of 2 lemons, grated
6 cloves
1 Tbsp. thyme
2 bay leaves
6 peppercorns, slightly crushed
salt to taste
2 lbs. fresh mushrooms, thickly sliced
2 Tbsps. lemon juice
1 tsp. dill weed

Combine White Zinfandel, olive oil, onions, lemon zest, cloves, thyme, bay leaves, peppercorns and salt in a medium saucepan. Bring to a boil. Lower heat and simmer 8 to 10 minutes. Strain. Return to a saucepan, large enough to hold mushrooms, and bring to a simmer. Add mushrooms and simmer until fork-tender, about 10 minutes. Pour into a bowl, cover and refrigerate for several hours or overnight. Just before serving, pour off marinade and mix in lemon juice and dill weed. Serves 8 to 10 as antipasto or 4 served on lettuce leaves as a salad. Chenin Blanc or Johannisberg Riesling may be substituted for White Zinfandel as long as the residual sugar doesn't exceed 1.5%.

White Bean Salad

This zesty bean salad can be a meal in itself served with hot garlic bread and a big bodied red wine.

Notes from Patti:

Fresh basil is a must for this dish. Basil is easy to grow even if you don't have a garden. It will grow very well in pots on your window sill and is a most attractive addition to the kitchen.

4 cups freshly cooked dried white kidney beans, well drained
3/4 cup olive oil
1/4 cup white wine vinegar
3 cloves garlic, finely minced
10 fresh basil leaves, finely minced
4 large ripe tomatoes
1 tsp. salt
Coarsely ground pepper to taste

Toss beans with olive oil, pepper, vinegar, garlic and basil. Set aside for several hours to marinate. Slice stem ends from tomatoes. Scoop out the seeds and discard. Scoop out and coarsely chop the pulp. Salt the shells pulp lightly. Invert the shells on paper towels and let drain. Drain the pulp in a sieve. Combine pulp with beans and mound the mixture in the tomato shells. Sprinkle with pepper. Serves 4.

Chilled Beet Salad

2–1 lb. cans julienne beets, drained
1/3 cup olive oil
1/4 cup white wine vinegar
2 Tbsps. dijon style mustard
2 Tbsps. caraway seeds
1 tsp. sugar
Salt and freshly ground pepper to taste
Lettuce leaves
4 green bell pepper rings

Notes from Patti:

This is a wonderful do ahead salad and can be doubled for large buffets. The beets can be marinated up to two days before serving. I sometimes garnish with grated hard cooked eggs.

In a jar with a tight fitting lid, combine oil, vinegar, mustard, caraway seeds, sugar and salt and pepper to taste. Shake thoroughly. Place beets in a large mixing bowl and toss with dressing. Cover and chill for several hours. Just before serving, line salad bowl with lettuce leaves. Add dressed beets and garnish with overlapping pepper rings. Serves 8.

Hot and Tangy Potato Salad

1/4 cup olive oil
2 Tbsps. red wine vinegar
1 Tbsp. Dijon mustard
Salt and pepper to taste
2 1/2 lbs. new potatoes
1/3 cup chopped parsley
1 cup chopped green onions, with some
  of the green stems
1 Tbsp. fresh chopped cilantro

In a small jar with a lid, combine oil, vinegar, mustard, and salt and pepper to taste. Shake thoroughly and set aside. Place potatoes in a large pot and cover with water. Bring to a boil, cover and cook until fork-tender; about 15 to 20 minutes. Drain and cut into quarters into a large bowl. Pour dressing over warm potatoes. Sprinkle with green onions, parsley and cilantro. Toss and serve at once. Serves 6.

Green Salad with Gorgonzola Cheese

Gorgonzola cheese is probably my favorite cheese from anywhere in the world. It makes a simple green salad a special treat.

6 Tbsps. olive oil
2 Tbsps. red wine vinegar
1 Tbsp. lemon juice
1/4 tsp. salt
Freshly ground black pepper to taste
8 to 10 cups mixed salad greens such as romaine and
*   bibb lettuce, watercress and radicchio washed and torn*
*   into pieces and thoroughly dried with paper toweling.*
*   Chill.*
6 oz. Gorgonzola cheese, crumbled.

In a jar with a tight fitting lid combine oil, vinegar, lemon juice, salt and pepper. Cover and thoroughly shake. Combine greens in a large salad bowl and toss with dressing. Add cheese and toss again. Serves 8.

Nicoise Salad

I could not complete this chapter without the inclusion of my version of the classic Salad Nicoise–and there are many versions! This salad is named for those wonderful Nicoise olives and no substitute is possible for them.

3/4 cup olive oil
1/4 cup red wine vinegar
1 heaping tablespoon Dijon style mustard
4 to 5 sprigs parsley
1 tsp. sugar
Salt and freshly ground black pepper to taste (about 1/2 teaspoon each)
1 head bibb lettuce, washed and thoroughly dried. Refrigerated
8 new potatoes, scrubbed
1 lb. fresh green beans, steamed until tender but still crisp
1 small red onion, thinly sliced and separated into rings
1/4 cup parsley, minced
4 large ripe tomatoes, cored and quartered
4 hard cooked eggs, shelled and quartered
1–6 1/2 oz. can white tuna packed in water, drained and flaked
16 Nicoise olives

Notes from Patti:

This recipe can easily be doubled or even tripled for a buffet or picnic. For this purpose, line a large platter with lettuce leaves. Toss all ingredients, except eggs and olives, with vinaigrette and arrange on the platter and garnish with eggs and olives.

Place olive oil, vinegar, mustard, sugar, parsley and salt and pepper in the bowl of a food processor fitted with a steel blade and blend until smooth. Scrape down once or twice. Pour into small bowl and set aside. Cook potatoes in boiling salted water until tender, about 10 to 12 minutes. Cool enough to handle and quarter. Place potatoes, green beans, onion rings and parsley in a large bowl. Gently toss with half the vinaigrette and refrigerate until chilled. Line 4 luncheon plates with chilled lettuce leaves. Divide green beans into 4 equal bundles and place on lettuce. Add equal amounts of potatoes and onion rings to each plate. Alternate tomatoes and hard cooked egg around plate, (1 tomato and 1 egg per plate). Sprinkle equal amounts of tuna over each plate and garnish with olives. Drizzle remaining vinegarette over each salad. Cover with plastic wrap and refrigerate for an hour or more. Serves 4.

Soup

I don't exactly abhor canned soups but neither do I applaud them. Certainly they are convenient and yes they are easy, but they lack memories. Memories of cold blustery days, when rain pelted the windows and fog drifted in like unfriendly ghosts. On those days Grandma would always take out her big copper kettle and make soup. I would ask her what kind of soup we would make because I know that would provoke a wonderful game of improvisation. Each ingredient had to be discussed and decisions made. There were questions of how beans were dried and remembrances of hot summer days when we had put the tomatoes in jars, that now became a part of our soup. We were cheered by the warmth of the fire and knew there was no need to hurry this day. You see, Grandma knew soup comforted one's soul as much as one's body. You don't get that out of a can!

Blanc de Noir Onion Soup

Onion soup is as varied as the cultures of the world. There is no "classic" so to speak. I have tried many versions over the years and I like this one the best.

2 medium white onions, coarsely chopped
4 Tbsps. butter
Pinch of cinnamon
5 cups beef stock
2 cups Blanc de Noir sparkling wine
6 tsps. freshly grated Parmesan cheese
Salt and pepper to taste

In a large skillet, saute the onions in the butter until just transparent. Add cinnamon and stir. Transfer the onions to a large pot. Add beef stock and Blanc de Noir. Bring to boiling point, lower the heat and simmer 3 to 4 minutes. Top each serving with a teaspoon of cheese. Serves 6. You may substitute any dry sparkling wine for the Blanc de Noir.

Fresh Basil Soup

If God made anything better than food–He kept it to himself, and fresh basil is one of his more perfect creations. No matter how basil is used, especially in this soup, my mouth always says "more"! I'm sure you will like this soup as much as I do.

2 1/2 cups fresh basil
1/2 cup Italian parsley leaves (must be Italian parsley)
4 large cloves garlic
1/2 cup pine nuts
4 Tbsps. olive oil
2 Tbsps. butter
2 1/2 cups chicken stock, preferably homemade
1/2 cup Zinfandel
Salt and pepper to taste
1/4 cup freshly grated Parmesan cheese

In a food processor fitted with a steel blade, process basil, parsley and garlic until minced. Add pine nuts and process until nut are finely chopped. With machine running add olive oil and butter, process until all ingredients are well blended. Pour chicken stock and Zinfandel into a medium saucepan. Whisk in basil mixture and simmer over low heat for 20 minutes. Season with salt and pepper. Top each serving with Parmesan cheese. Serves 4. Merlot may be substituted for Zinfandel.

Slow Cooking Minestrone

This is so easy you can put it together before you go to work in the morning. This is so good and hearty, all you need is a salad, sourdough bread and a good bottle of wine!

1 lb. lean beef, cubed
1 tsp. salt
1/8 tsp. pepper
1 bay leaf
1 Tbsp. parsley flakes
1 tsp. oregano
1/2 cup dry white beans
1 large carrot, thinly sliced
1 large onion diced
1–16oz. can Italian plum tomatoes, broken up
1 cup uncooked vermicelli
3 cups water
1 cup fresh or frozen baby peas
3/4 lb. mushrooms, sliced thick
1/2 cup dry sherry

Place beef in bottom of slow cooker. Add remaining ingredients, except peas, mushrooms and sherry. Stir to mix, cover and cook, on low setting, 8-10 hours. Turn to highest heat setting, add mushrooms, peas and sherry. Cover and cook another 1/2 hour. Serve with freshly grated Parmesan cheese. 6 hearty servings. No substitute for dry sherry.

Hot Italian Sausage Soup

A big green salad, fresh sourdough bread, the rest of the Petite Sirah, fresh fruit and cheese and you have a party!

1 lb. hot Italian sausage, cut in 1/2" slices
6 cloves garlic, minced
2 large onions, coarsely chopped
1–16 oz can Italian plum tomatoes
4 cups beef stock
2 cups Petite Sirah
1/2 tsp. basil
1/2 tsp. thyme
A big pinch hot red pepper flakes
3 Tbsps. chopped parsley
3 medium zucchini, sliced
3 cups uncooked farfalle pasta
8 Tbsps. freshly grated Parmesan cheese

Notes from Patti:

I make this soup the day before I serve it in order to allow the flavors to marry. It also freezes very well.

In a large dutch oven, brown sausage over medium heat. Drain fat. Add garlic and onions and cook until onions are transparent. Stir in and break up tomatoes. Add beef stock, Petite Sirah, basil, thyme, pepper flakes and parsley. Simmer uncovered for 30 minutes. Add zucchini and pasta and simmer an additional 20 minutes. Top each serving with a tablespoon of Parmesan cheese. Serves 8. Cabernet Sauvignon may be substituted for Petite Sirah.

Cream of Squash Soup

2 lbs. yellow crookneck squash, cut in 2" pieces
1/2 cup chicken stock
1 oz. crystalized ginger
2 1/2 cup heavy cream
3 Tbsps. brandy
1/8 tsp. ground mace
Salt and freshly ground pepper to taste

Boil squash 10 minutes. Drain well and pat dry with paper toweling. Put squash, stock and ginger in a food processor bowl fitted with a steel blade. Process until smooth. Pour into a heavy saucepan. Whisk in cream, brandy and mace. Warm over medium heat. Season with salt and pepper. Serves 6.

Cream of Cauliflower Soup

4 Tbsps. butter
1/4 cup all-purpose flour
4 cups chicken stock
4 cups dry vermouth
1 medium cauliflower, separated into flowerettes
1/4 tsp. ground nutmeg
1 cup cream

Melt butter over medium heat in a large Dutch oven. Mix in flour with a wooden spoon until smooth. Gradually add chicken stock and vermouth and stir until smooth. Add cauliflower, reserving 1 cup, to broth.. Bring to a boil, reduce heat and cover. Simmer 20 minutes or until cauliflower is tender. Pour into a food processor, fitted with a steel blade, and process until smooth. Return mixture to Dutch oven. Stir in reserved cauliflower and bring back to a boil. Cover, reduce heat and simmer 10 minutes. Stir in cream and sprinkle with nutmeg. Serves 6.

Quick and Easy Mushroom Consomme

1/2 cup dry vermouth
1 lb. mushrooms, thickly sliced
6 cups beef stock
4 fresh green onions, sliced with 1" green stems
1/2 tsp. dried tarragon
2 Tbsps. fresh lemon juice
Salt and freshly ground black pepper
4 paper thin lemon slices

Notes from Patti:

This soup can easily be doubled or even tripled.

In a medium saucepan, bring vermouth to a simmer. Add mushrooms and simmer until liquid is almost evaporated, about 10 minutes. Add beef stock, onions and tarragon. Cover and simmer 30 minutes. Season with lemon juice, salt and pepper. Garnish each serving with lemon slice. Serves 4. No substitute for dry vermouth.

Buttermilk Zucchini Soup

2 medium zucchini, sliced
1 1/2 cups chicken broth
4 green onions, minced with part of green stems
1 clove garlic, finely minced
3/4 cup. buttermilk
1/4 cup dry sherry
1/2 tsp. dill weed
6 tsps. sour cream

In a medium saucepan, combine zucchini, chicken broth, onions and garlic, simmer until zucchini is tender. Pour into food processor fitted with a steel blade, or blender and process until smooth. Add buttermilk, dry sherry and dill weed and blend. Return to saucepan and heat. Spoon into serving bowl and top each serving with a teaspoon of sour cream. Serves 6. Dry vermouth may be substituted for the dry sherry.

Shrimp Bisque

This is an elegant way to start a dinner party and takes just minutes to make.

Notes from Patti:

If using a blender to process shrimp, process in 3 batches.

1 1/2 lbs. small shrimp, cleaned and deveined
1 cup water
1 lb. fresh mushrooms, half thinly sliced and the rest
  finely chopped
2 Tbsps. butter
1/2 cup all-purpose flour
1 cup Sauvignon Blanc
1 chicken bouillon cube
1 Tbsp. lemon juice
1/8 tsp. nutmeg
2 cups heavy cream
3 Tbsps. dry vermouth

Put shrimp and water in a food processor, fitted with a steel blade and process until finely chopped. Set aside. In a large saucepan, saute mushrooms in butter until liquid evaporates. Stir in flour to coat mushrooms. Slowly stir in Sauvignon Blanc. Add bouillon cube, lemon juice, nutmeg and shrimp mixture. Simmer covered, about 10 minutes. Stir often. Add cream and dry vermouth. Heat thoroughly, being careful not to boil. Serves 6. Fume Blanc may be substituted for Sauvignon Blanc.

Mussel Soup

4 lbs. fresh mussels
4–8oz. bottles clam juice
1 cup Chardonnay
1 large bunch parsley, coarsely chopped
10 cloves garlic, finely minced
1/2 cup butter
1 large white onion, coarsely chopped
2 large carrots, coarsely chopped
4 ribs celery, coarsely, chopped
1 tsp. fennel seed
1/2 tsp. thyme
2 cups heavy cream

Scrub mussels with stiff brush under cold running water. With a small, sharp knife, remove and discard "beards", the small black tufts attached to the shells. In a large saucepan, bring 1 bottle of clam juice, Chardonnay, parsley and garlic to a boil. Add mussels, cover and steam 5 minutes or until shells open. Remove mussels from broth with a slotted spoon. Cool until easy to handle, then remove mussels from shells and set aside. Reserve broth. In a large saucepan melt butter. Add onions, carrots and celery and saute until tender. Add remaining clam juice, fennel seed and thyme. Simmer 15 minutes. Add reserved broth. Puree and strain through fine wire mesh or cheese cloth and heat through. Serves 6. Sauvignon Blanc may be substituted for Chardonnay.

Potato and Leek Soup

This is one of my favorite soups. Not only because it is delicious and filling, but because it is fast and easy to make and the ingredients are usually on hand.

4 cups chicken stock
2 medium potatoes, diced
1 medium white onion, diced
1 leek, diced
3 Tbsps. butter
3 Tbsps. flour
1 3/4 cups milk
1/4 cup dry sherry
Salt and white pepper to taste

Notes from Patti:

Leeks belong to the onion family and have a slightly garlic flavor. Unfortunately, leeks are rather expensive in this country. A good substitute is a medium white onion diced with 3 cloves of garlic.

Bring chicken stock to a boil. Add potatoes, onions and leeks. Reduce heat and simmer, covered, until vegetables are tender crisp. Melt butter in a saucepan. Stir in flour and cook over low heat for 2 to 3 minutes, stirring constantly. Do not allow the mixture to brown; heat milk and dry sherry and add it to the butter and flour mixture, whisking until the mixture is smooth and slightly thicker. Add chicken stock and vegetables and season with salt and pepper. Serves 4 to 6. Dry vermouth may be substituted for dry sherry.

Easy Three Bean Soup

Many foods taste better the day after they have been prepared. This is especially true of dried beans. I always make this the day before I want to serve it.

8 cups chicken stock
4 large onions, coarsely diced
4 large carrots, cut into fourths
4 stalks celery, cut into fourths
3/4 cup dried lentils
3/4 cup dried split peas
3/4 cup dried north white beans
4 hot Italian sausages, cut in 1/4" slices
Salt and pepper to taste
1/2 cup dry vermouth

Notes from Patti:

Vermouth is made with herbs and adds an herbal taste to this wonderful hearty soup.

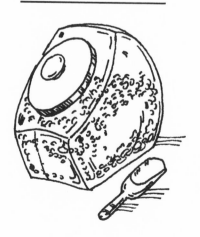

Combine all ingredients, except dry vermouth, in a large pot and simmer, covered, until white beans are tender. Adjust seasonings and stir in dry vermouth. Serves 8. No substitute for dry vermouth.

Clam Chowder (Not Just Another Soup!)

Notes from Patti:

I've seen lots of recipes titled "A Meal In A Pot"— this has to be the original. Served with a simple green salad and lots of sourdough bread for dipping...What more could you want? A glass of California Chardonnay to drink with it!

4 strips lean bacon, sliced in 1/4" pieces
3 cloves garlic, finely minced
1 large onion, coarsely chopped
2 stalks celery, chopped, including leaves
1 medium green bell pepper, stemmed, seeded and ribs
  removed, chopped
1–#2 can Italian plum tomatoes, with juice
6 large russet potatoes, peeled and cubed
1 tsp. salt
1 tsp. freshly ground black pepper
1/4 tsp. cayenne pepper
1 tsp. dried basil
1 tsp. dried thyme
2 tsps. Worcestershire sauce
2/3 cup Chardonnay
2–6 oz cans minced clams, with juice
3 cups boiling water

Saute bacon in a large Dutch oven until transparent. Add garlic and onions and cook until bacon is golden. Add celery, green peppers, and potatoes. Add tomatoes and break up with wooden spoon. Add salt, pepper, cayenne pepper, basil, thyme, Worcestershire, sauce. and Chardonnay. Add clam juice and boiling water and stir. Cover and simmer 30 minutes. Add clams and simmer an additional 10 minutes. Serves 6 as main course. No substitute for Chardonnay.

Vegetables

I love vegetables! All kinds of vegetables-well, I guess I don't really love okra, but I love rutabagas pureed with a bit of butter and cream and a dollop of sweet vermouth. Glazed pearl onions set my mouth watering. How could one cook without the regal potato? Or fresh green beans and snow peas? The taste and color of a baby carrot just out of the ground is unsurpassed. The delicate shading of young, tender lettuce reminds one of the paintings of Cezanne. Awakening senses of sight and even smell. No matter what is prepared for Easter Dinner, the first asparagus of the year is anticipated as the first flowers. I live on garden fresh vegetables during the summer and in the middle of winter, yearn for a vine ripe tomato (the closest I've ever come to that flavor are sun dried tomatoes–wonderful)! The thought of just picked corn makes me smile and stuffed zucchini topped with fresh sauce brings back memories of childhood–memories of sitting on the front porch shelling fresh peas with grandma on a beautiful summer afternoon.

How to Prepare and Cook Artichokes

Cut off stems at base of artichokes, turn on side and cut off the top of the artichoke. Remove tough outer leaves. Starting with bottom leaves, snip off the top of each leaf with sharp kitchen shears. Stand artichokes upright in a deep saucepan large enough for the artichokes to fit snugly in the pan. Add 3" boiling water, 11/2 teaspoons salt, 2 tablespoons olive oil and 1 tablespoon fresh lemon juice. Cover and bring to a boil. Lower heat and simmer gently for 30 to 40 minutes or until the base can be pierced easily. Invert artichokes on paper toweling and drain. Gently spread the center leaves and scrap out the choke.

Artichokes Cooked in Wine

I can already see some of you shouting about using your best Gewurztraminer in a vegetable. But just wait until you taste these artichokes! The citrusy flavor of the wine blends perfectly with the artichokes.

> *4 large artichokes*
> *Salt and pepper to taste*
> *1 tsp. dried marjoram*
> *3 cloves garlic, minced*
> *6 green onions, sliced with 1" of green stems*
> *2 cups chicken stock*
> *3/4 cup Gewurztraminer*
> *3 Tbsp. olive oil*

Trim tops and bottoms of artichokes and snip pointed ends of leaves with kitchen scissors. Cut in half and remove choke. Place in a large pot. Sprinkle with salt and pepper. Add marjoram, garlic and green onions. Add chicken stock and Gewurztraminer. Dribble oil over top. Cover pot and bring to a boil. Reduce heat and simmer 45 minutes to an hour until tender. Remove artichokes with slotted spoon to a platter and keep warm. Strain stock and pour into a small saucepan. Bring to a boil and reduce to half. Serve sauce with artichokes. Serves 4. Johannisberg Riesling may be substituted for Gewurztraminer, but I like the Gewurztraminer better.

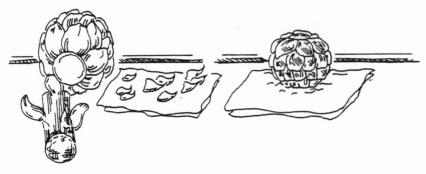

Stuffed Artichokes

These artichokes are delicious hot or cold, and I often make extras to tuck into lunch boxes.

4 medium artichokes, prepared by basic directions
1/3 cup olive oil
1 small white onion, finely chopped
1 cup finely chopped parsley
1 cup thinly sliced celery
2 large cloves garlic, minced
1/3 cup Sauvignon Blanc
3 cups coarse, fresh bread crumbs
1/2 cup freshly grated parmesan cheese
1/2 tsp. oregano
Salt and freshly ground black pepper
Additional Parmesan cheese
Additional olive oil

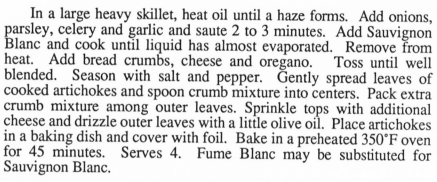

In a large heavy skillet, heat oil until a haze forms. Add onions, parsley, celery and garlic and saute 2 to 3 minutes. Add Sauvignon Blanc and cook until liquid has almost evaporated. Remove from heat. Add bread crumbs, cheese and oregano. Toss until well blended. Season with salt and pepper. Gently spread leaves of cooked artichokes and spoon crumb mixture into centers. Pack extra crumb mixture among outer leaves. Sprinkle tops with additional cheese and drizzle outer leaves with a little olive oil. Place artichokes in a baking dish and cover with foil. Bake in a preheated 350°F oven for 45 minutes. Serves 4. Fume Blanc may be substituted for Sauvignon Blanc.

Artichokes Stuffed with Creamed Spinach

6 prepared artichokes, dechoked
1–10 oz. package frozen chopped spinach
1–3oz. brick of cream cheese, room temperature
3 fresh green onions, white part only, finely minced
2 Tbsps. dry sherry
1/4 tsp. nutmeg
Salt and pepper to taste

Cook spinach according to directions on package and drain. Place in a terry kitchen towel and squeeze dry as possible. Cream spinach, cream cheese, onions, dry sherry, and nutmeg in a food processor fitted with a plastic blade. Season with salt and pepper. Fill prepared artichokes with mixture and chill. To eat, pull off a leaf and dip into the mixture. Serves 6. Dry vermouth may be substituted for dry sherry.

Cream Corn Frittata

This is one of those old standby dishes that fits todays life style.

6 large eggs, beaten
1–17 oz. can cream style corn
1–4 oz can green chilies, drained and coarsely chopped
3 Tbsp. dry sherry
1 1/2 cups extra sharp Cheddar cheese, shredded
1 1/2 cups Monterey Jack cheese, shredded
1 tsp. Worcestershire sauce
1/4 tsp. freshly ground black pepper

In a large bowl combine all ingredients and beat until well blended. Pour into a buttered baking dish. Bake in a preheated 325°F oven 1 hour or until firm and slightly browned on top. Serves 8 to 10 as antipasto or 6 as a luncheon dish. Serve hot or cold. Dry vermouth may be substituted for dry sherry.

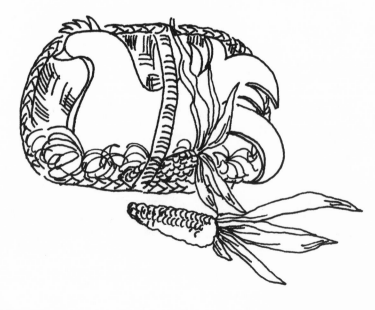

Onion and Pepper Frittata

2 Tbsps. olive oil
1 Tbsp. butter
1 large white onion, thinly sliced
1 large clove garlic
2 medium green bell peppers, stemmed, seeded and
*   ribs removed and cut into thin strips*
2 medium red bell peppers, stemmed, seeded and ribs
*   removed and cut into thin strips*
2 Tbsps. sweet vermouth
1/2 tsp. crushed cumin
1/2 tsp. coriander
Salt and freshly ground black pepper to taste
4 large eggs
1/2 cup sour cream
1 cup plain yogurt
1/2 lb. Cheddar cheese, sliced
Paprika

Notes from Patti:

Frittatas are really a meal all by themselves, but since vegetables play such an important part in this presentation, I have included it in this chapter. This has always been one of my favorite luncheon dishes.

In a large heavy skillet, heat oil until haze forms. Add butter, onions and garlic and saute until onions are transparent. Add peppers and vermouth. Add cumin, coriander and season with salt and pepper. Set aside. In a medium mixing bowl, combine eggs, sour cream and yogurt and whisk until mixture is smooth. Spread half the onion mixture on the bottom of a buttered ovenproof casserole. Cover with half the slices of cheese. Repeat layering. Pour egg mixture over all. Sprinkle with paprika. Bake, uncovered, 30 to 40 minutes or until set. Serves 6. No substitute for sweet vermouth.

Yams in Port Sauce

This is truly an elegant dish and complements simply prepared ham and pork.

1 gallon cold water
1 tsp. salt
2 lbs. yams, peeled and shredded
1/4 cup sugar
1/2 cup light corn syrup
1/4 cup port
1/4 cup butter (must be butter)
1 cup unsweetened pineapple juice
Freshly grated nutmeg

Preheat oven to 350°F. Butter 9x13 inch baking dish. Combine 1 gallon cold water with salt in a large pot. Stir in yams and let stand 1 minute. Drain thoroughly and arrange in prepared dish. Heat sugar, corn syrup and port in a large heavy saucepan over low heat until sugar dissolves, swirling pan occasionally. Increase heat and boil until sauce is the consistency of heavy cream, about 6-8 minutes. Remove from heat and stir in butter until melted. Pour pineapple juice over yams and drizzle with port sauce. Sprinkle with nutmeg and bake 1 hour. Serves 8. Use either a Tinta Madera or tawny port. There is no substitute for port.

Notes from Patti:

Stirring any vegetables high in starch, like yams, into cold salted water helps remove excessive starch.

Sherry Zucchini Combo

1 medium white onion, diced
2 cloves garlic, finely minced
1 Tbsp. olive oil
1 Tbsp. butter
3 to 4 medium zucchini, thickly sliced
3/4 lb. fresh mushrooms, thickly sliced
1 large tomato, peeled, seeded and cut into eights
Dash nutmeg
2 Tbsps. dry sherry

Heat oil and butter in a large skillet. Saute onions and garlic until onions are transparent. Add zucchini and mushrooms and cook until zucchini are tender-crisp. Stir in tomato, nutmeg and sherry and cook until tomatoes are heated. Serves 4. Dry vermouth may be substituted for the dry sherry.

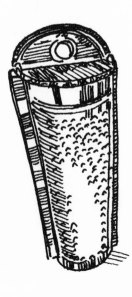

Stuffed Zucchini

Just about the time your family says NO MORE ZUCCHINI, surprise them with this flavor combination. Even kids like them!

6 small zucchinis
3 small carrots, quartered
2 Tbsps. butter
1/2 tsp. white pepper
2 Tbsps. cream
2 Tbsps. cream sherry
2 Tbsps. butter, melted
4 Tbsps. fresh bread crumbs
4 Tbsps. Parmesan cheese, freshly grated

Notes from Patti:

You can prepare these zucchinis up to the point of the bread crumbs and cheese the day before serving. If you don't have a pastry bag, carefully spoon carrot mixture into the shells.

Drop zucchini in 3 quarts salted water and boil for 3 minutes. Drain and set aside. Cook carrots in small amount of salted water and drain. In a processor bowl fitted with a steel blade, process carrots, butter, pepper, cream and sherry until smooth. Scrape into a small bowl and set aside. Cut cooked zucchini in halves lengthwise and carefully scoop out centers with a melon baller. Brush zucchini with melted butter. Fit pastry bag with small metal tip. Spoon carrot mixture into bag and pipe into zucchini. Top each zucchini half with bread crumbs. Sprinkle with cheese. Place zucchini in shallow ovenproof baking pan. Bake in a preheated 350°F oven for 15 minutes. Serves 6. No substitute for cream sherry.

Herbed Zucchini

2 medium zucchini, sliced
1 small white onion, sliced
2 Tbsps. olive oil
2 Tbsps. chopped fresh mint
1 dash angostura bitters
3 Tbsps. French Colombard

Heat oil in a large heavy skillet until haze forms. Add zucchini and onions and saute 3 to 4 minutes, stirring constantly to prevent over-browning. Add mint, bitters and French Colombard and simmer 2 to 3 additional minutes covered, or until zucchini is tender. Serves 4.

Spinach Timbales

Notes from Patti:

Timbales are wonderfully versatile—they can be prepared in individual molds or a larger 4 cup mold. They are good hot or cold. They are great for brunch. Serve them with a sauce made of 1 cup of cream fraiche and 2 – 3 teaspoons of prepared horseradish.

2 lbs. fresh spinach
4 Tbsps. butter
1/2 cup onion, finely minced
2 Tbsps. dry vermouth
Salt and pepper to taste
1 1/2 cups cream
4 large eggs, well beaten
1/2 cup grated Cheddar cheese

Wash spinach and remove stems. Cook in as little water as possible for 3 minutes or until tender. Drain and chop. Place in a kitchen towel and squeeze out as much liquid as possible. Melt butter in a large skillet and saute onions until soft. Add dry vermouth and cook until alcohol has burned off. Stir in spinach and salt and pepper. Add cream and beaten eggs. Stir in cheese. Divide mixture between 8–10 ounce buttered custard cups. Arrange molds in a large pan and add boiling water to reach half way up the side of molds. Bake in a preheated 325°F oven 20 to 30 minutes. Unmold and serve at once. Serves 8. A good dry sherry may be substituted for dry vermouth.

Vegetables Madeira

I have always liked combining vegetables because you can create almost any color and texture you want. It's also fun to combine different varieties of the same vegetable.

2 Tbsps. butter
1/2 cup Madeira
4 small turnips, peeled and cut in 1/8" slices
8 celery stalks, halved lengthwise and cut into 3" pieces
8 small carrots, peeled and cut in half
8 fresh green onions, trimmed and cut in half
Salt and freshly ground black pepper to taste

Melt the butter in a large heavy skillet over low heat. Whisk in Madeira and increase heat. Bring to a boil. Add vegetables and toss to coat. Lower heat, cover and cook about 15 minutes or until vegetables are tender. Season with salt and pepper to taste. Serves 8. Dry vermouth may be substituted for the Madeira, however the Madeira lends a "nutty" flavor. Dry vermouth will lend an herbal flavor.

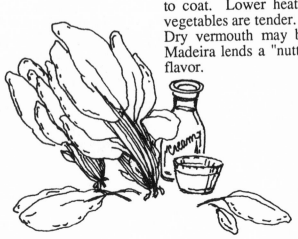

Sauvignon Blanc Broccoli

1/4 cup olive oil
2 large cloves garlic, finely chopped
1 large bunch broccoli, cut into flowerettes
1 1/2 cups Sauvignon Blanc
Salt and freshly ground pepper

In a heavy skillet, heat oil until haze forms. Remove skillet from heat and add the garlic to the oil. Stir for 30 seconds, return skillet and lower heat. Add broccoli and toss until broccoli is coated with oil. Add Sauvignon Blanc, salt and pepper. Simmer, uncovered, for 5 minutes. Cover and simmer 15 minutes. Transfer broccoli to a heated bowl with a slotted spoon. Boil the liquid in the skillet over high heat until reduced to 1/2 cup. Pour over broccoli and serve. Serves 6. Fume Blanc may be substituted for the Sauvignon Blanc.

Notes from Patti:

Don't throw away the broccoli stalks! Peel the stalks, slice and cook in 4 cups of chicken stock until tender. Pour into a food processor and puree. Return to the pot. Add 1 cup cream, season with salt and freshly ground black pepper and heat through. You have 4 cups delicious broccoli soup.

Candied Carrots

People who don't like carrots love these carrots! They are great for dinner parties because the carrots and sauce can be prepared early in the day and finished just before serving.

8 medium sized carrots, peeled and cut into 1" lengths
4 Tbsps. butter
1/4 cup brown sugar
1/8 tsp. ground cinnamon
1/4 cup tawny port

Place carrots in a saucepan and cover with water. Cook just until tender but crisp. Drain. In a large heavy skillet, melt butter. Add brown sugar and cinnamon and stir until sugar melts. Add carrots and toss until carrots are coated. Add port and simmer 5 minutes, stirring occasionally. Serves 4.

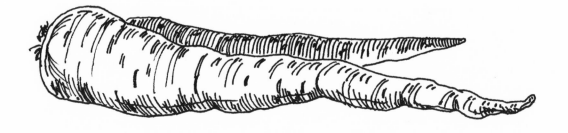

My Favorite Mushrooms

It takes no longer to prepare these mushrooms than to broil a steake or lamb chop and they add so much flavor. Fold them into an omelet or top fluffy scrambled eggs with them. No matter what you serve them with they are delivered.

2 Tbsps. olive oil
2 Tbsps. butter
1 lb. fresh mushrooms, thickly sliced
4 large cloves garlic, minced
1/4 cup dry sherry
2 Tbsps. parsley, chopped
Salt and freshly ground black pepper to taste

In a large heavy skillet, heat oil until a haze forms. Add butter and mushrooms. Saute 2 to 3 minutes. Add garlic and sherry and cook until liquid has evaporated. Add parsley and toss. Season with salt and pepper. Serves 4. Dry vermouth may be substituted for the dry sherry.

Mushroom Stuffed Tomatoes

I wait for the first vine ripened tomatoes of the season for this dish. It is a refreshing lunch served with a green salad and the rest of the Colombard.

1 Tbsp. salt
6 large ripe tomatoes, tops sliced off and seeded
1 Tbsp. olive oil
1 Tbsp. butter
1 lb. mushrooms, thinly sliced
1/2 cup minced parsley
1/4 cup French Colombard
3 large cloves garlic, finely minced
1/3 cup fresh bread crumbs
1/4 cup freshly grated Parmesan cheese
1/2 Tbsp. dill weed (I like more)
2-3 Tbsps. cream

Sprinkle the tomatoes with salt and invert onto paper toweling to drain. In a large heavy skillet, heat oil until haze forms. Add butter. Add mushrooms and cook until soft, stirring occasionally, about 10 minutes. Add parsley, French Colombard, and garlic. Reduce heat and cook until almost all liquid evaporates. Set aside and cool. Position rack in upper third of oven and preheat to 400°F. In a mixing bowl, combine bread crumbs, cheese and dill weed. Toss with oil and cream to moisten. Divide mushroom mixture among tomato shells. Sprinkle with bread crumbs. Arrange in 8" square baking dish. Bake until the crumbs are golden brown, 10 to 15 minutes. Serves 6. You may substitute Fume Blanc for French Colombard.

Green Beans Almondine

2 lbs. fresh green beans, ends snipped off
  and strings removed
4 Tbsps. butter
1/2 lb. fresh mushrooms, thickly sliced
1/4 cup dry sherry
1/2 cup slivered almonds
Few grinds black pepper

Steam green beans until tender crisp, about 10 minutes. Drain and set aside. Melt 2 tablespoons butter in a large heavy skillet. Saute mushrooms 2 to 3 minutes. Add dry sherry and simmer until liquid evaporates. In a small skillet melt the remaining butter and saute almonds until brown. Toss green beans and almonds in skillet with mushrooms and heat. Sprinkle with pepper. Serves 6. Dry Madeira or dry vermouth may be substituted for dry sherry.

Notes from Patti:

These green beans make a great salad. Simply toss with vinaigrette dressing and chill. Serve on lettuce leaves and garnish with cherry tomatoes.

Lemony Green Beans

If you are fortunate enough to have a vegetable garden then you know how delicious freshly picked green beans can be. I think the combination of citrus and sherry gives these green beans a special flavor.

1 lb. fresh green beans, ends and strings removed,
  broken in half
1 Tbsp. olive oil
1 Tbsp. butter
1 celery rib, cut lengthwise and diced
8 large mushrooms, thickly sliced
1 large clove garlic, minced
2 Tbsps. dry sherry
1 tsp. grated lemon peel
2 Tbsps. fresh lemon juice
1/4 tsp. dill weed (I like more)
Salt and freshly ground black pepper to taste
1 whole pimento, minced

Steam green beans in a small amount of water until tender crisp, about 5 minutes. Set aside. In a large heavy skillet heat oil until haze forms. Add butter, celery, mushrooms, garlic and dry sherry. Saute until mushrooms are brown. Add green beans and toss. Stir in lemon peel, lemon juice and dill weed. Season with salt and pepper. Transfer to serving bowl and garnish with pimento. Serves 6. No substitute for dry sherry. It lends a nutty taste to the beans that taste terrific.

Tomatoes Stuffed with Peas and Tuna

On one of those hot days when you really don't want to cook. This is so easy to put together and satisfying to the palate.

6 medium fresh tomatoes
1–10 oz. package frozen baby peas, defrosted and
thoroughly drained, set aside
1–6 1/2 oz. can tuna, packed in water, drained,
flaked and set aside
1 medium cucumber, peeled, halved, seeded,
coarsely chopped
3/4 cup mayonnaise
3/4 cup sour cream
1 tsp. sugar
1 Tbsp. white wine vinegar
1 Tbsp. fresh lemon juice
1/4 cup fresh mint, chopped
Salt and freshly ground black pepper to taste
A few sprigs of mint

Slice tops off tomatoes and seed. With a small melon baller, remove the sections. Insert on paper toweling and drain. In a large mixing bowl, gently toss peas, tuna and cucumbers. Place mayonnaise, sour cream, sugar, vinegar, lemon juice and mint in food processor fitted with a steel blade and process until smooth. Season with salt and pepper. Pour dressing over pea mixture and toss until well coated. Fill tomatoes with mixture. Garnish with mint sprig and chill for several hours before serving. Serves 6.

Eggplant Parmesana

Everyone loves eggplant parmesana, even if they don't like eggplant! This is even better if you make the sauce 2 to 3 days before assembling.

2 Tbsps. olive oil
2 Tbsps. butter
1 medium white onion, coarsely diced
3 cloves garlic, minced
1–1lb. can Italian plum tomatoes, drained, seeded and
  coarsely chopped
2 1/2 cups Merlot
2 tsps. fresh oregano, minced
2 Tbsps. fresh basil, minced
Salt and freshly ground black pepper to taste
1 large eggplant, cut into 1/2" thick slices
1/4 cup all-purpose flour
1/2 tsp. salt
1/8 tsp freshly ground black pepper
1/4 cup olive oil
1/2 cup freshly grated Parmesan cheese
1 slice mozzarella cheese

Notes from Patti:

This is much different than the eggplant parmesana in my last book "Wine In Everyday Cooking."

In a large heavy saucepan, heat oil until haze forms. Add butter, onions and garlic. Saute until onions are transparent. Add tomatoes, Merlot, oregano and basil. Bring to a boil and season with salt and pepper. Reduce heat and simmer, uncovered, 15 minutes. Stir occasionally. Combine flour, salt and pepper and dredge eggplant in mixture. Set aside. In a large heavy skillet hat oil until haze forms. Brown eggplant slices, on both sides, a few at a time. Add more oil as needed. Remove slices and drain on paper toweling. Preheat oven to 350°F. Spoon half the sauce into a shallow 10" baking dish. Arrange eggplant slices, overlapping and spoon sauce remaining sauce on top. Sprinkle with Parmesan and top with mozzarella slices. Bake 25 minutes or until mozzarella is golden. Serves 8. Pinot Noir may be substituted for Merlot.

Port Cabbage

Jim and Imogene Prager of Prager Winery in St. Helena, are among the nicest people I know. Their winery is tiny but they turn out some of the best California Port I've ever had the pleasure to taste. Their children there are seven of them–all help. I suggest when you are in St. Helena you stop by and have a taste of one of their wonderful ports and say hello for me!

Notes from Patti:

This cabbage may be served hot or cold. I like it better the second day and love it as a picnic food with ham sandwiches.

2 Tbsps.butter
1 medium white onion, diced
1 medium to large red cabbage
1 cup mango chutney, diced
3/4 cup tawny port
1/4 cup cider vinegar
3 Tbsps. brown sugar
Salt to taste

Melt butter in a large skillet over medium heat. Add onions and saute until transparent. Reduce heat to low and add remaining ingredients. Cover and simmer 25 to 30 minutes until cabbage is tender and liquid is reduced. Serves 6. Any type of port, such as Tinta Madera, may be substituted for the tawny port.

Grandma's Potatoes Italiano

These are my favorite baked potatoes, the flavor combination is probably unlike anything you have tasted. Once you try them they will become one of your favorites.

6 baking potatoes, scrubbed and baked
2 Tbsps. olive oil
2 Tbsps. butter
1/2 lb. fresh mushrooms, thinly sliced
6 fresh green onions, white part only, coarsely chopped
6 medium size fresh basil leaves, coarsely chopped
1 whole pimento, drained and coarsely chopped
2 Tbsps. dry sherry
Salt and pepper to taste

Notes from Patti:

If cholesterol is a problem eliminate butter and increase olive oil to 4 tablespoons. I often use olive oil simply because I like the flavor a little better.

In a large heavy skillet, heat oil until a haze forms. Add butter and mushrooms and toss until mushrooms are coated. Add onions and saute until mushrooms are brown. Add basil, pimento and dry sherry. Cook 2 to 3 minutes. Using a pot holder to protect your hands, lightly roll potatoes under your hand to soften. Press the ends ups. Spoon mushroom mixture over potatoes. Serves 6. No substitute for dry sherry.

Asparagus with Mustard Sauce

I don't think I will ever have all the asparagus I want, I've certainly had all I wanted at one meal–and all I wanted in a season. My problem is I want it in December and January and I can only get it in can or frozen–that is not acceptable to my palate. I want it fresh from the ground. This is one of my favorite ways to serve this vegetable.

2 lbs. asparagus, cleaned and tied into bundles
1 hard cooked egg
1 raw egg yolk
2 tsps. Dijon style mustard
1/2 cup olive oil
1 Tbsp. white wine vinegar
2 tsps. fresh lemon juice
Salt and freshly ground black pepper to taste
1 pimento, finely minced

In a large pot, bring 4 cups salted water to a boil. Add asparagus and cook until tender, about 10 minutes. Drain and run under cold water. Set aside. Separate hard cooked egg and finely minced white and set aside. In a food processor fitted with a steel blade, process hard cooked yolk, raw yolk and mustard until smooth. With motor running slowly add olive oil, processing until thick and smooth. Blend in vinegar and lemon juice. Pour into small bowl and season with salt and pepper. Arrange asparagus on serving platter. Spoon sauce over asparagus, leaving tips exposed, and garnish with egg whites and pimento. Serves 6.

Pasta

Fresh Pasta has a completely different taste and texture from the dried packaged pasta. Fresh pasta isn't difficult to make, but, like the piano, it takes practice. The more often you make pasta, the better and faster you become, until you can make it without thinking about it. If you don't choose to learn to make pasta by hand, there are many types of pasta makers ranging from hand crank models to the more expensive electric models. There are some food processors that have pasta attachments. I have not personally used these attachments, but it is my understanding that they work very well. I am, however, well acquainted with the electric models and mine is fantastic! I make everything from tube pasta to spaghetti. I also make bread sticks, crackers, gnocchi (potato dumplings), and cookies. If you have a large family or do a lot of entertaining, the electric machine is for you.

People who are cooking fresh pasta for the first time are always amazed to see how quickly the pasta cooks. As a general rule, fresh flat pasta is done within 5-10 seconds after the water in which it has been dropped returns to a boil. Tube pasta takes a little longer, but not much. Dried pasta takes at least 3-4 minutes longer to cook.

Fresh pasta is more readily available today than ever. Many delicatessens, bakeries, and even Italian restaurants make fresh pasta daily for sale. On both the west and east coast there are specialty shops that make nothing but pasta. Whether you make it yourself or purchase fresh pasta, you will find it well worth the effort.

Techniques for Making and Cooking Handmade Pasta

All pasta doughs are made with a varing ratio of flour to eggs; the larger the proportion of eggs, the richer the pasta. It is best made with Semolina, a type of wheat flour. If Semolina flour is not available, by all means use unbleached all-purpose flour. Never use instant or self-rising flour, as these cause the pasta to separate and break apart during cooking. Temperature is also an important factor when making pasta. A moderate room temperature away from drafts is best. A marble slab is the ideal surface for making and rolling pasta, but any smooth surface with do. Pasta can be mixed directly on the work surface, the way I prefer, or in a large bowl. The technique is the same.

Pasta Dough

3 1/2 cups all-purpose flour
5 eggs, room temperature
1 Tbsp. olive oil (more if necessary to make dough
  cohesive, but dry)
1/2 tsp. salt

Pour flour on work surface, or into a large bowl and form a well in the center. Beat the eggs, olive oil and salt, pour into the well. Mix the flour, a little at a time, with your fingers, starting from inside the well until eggs and flour are well blended. Knead the dough, pressing it with the heel of your hand and folding it several times until the pasta becomes smooth and elastic. This takes about 10 minutes. Wrap the dough in a damp cloth and allow it to rest for 1/2 hour to 45 minutes.

Divide the dough in half, keeping the remaining half covered, to prevent drying. Lightly flour the work surface and begin by rolling the dough away from you, turning the dough one quarter and repeating the procedure so the dough keeps an even circular shape. If any section becomes sticky, dust very lightly with flour. Carefully stretch the dough as you roll it and roll until it is almost paper thin. Roll up the dough on your rolling pin and unroll on a clean, dry cloth. Place it on the work surface (a little will hang over the edge.)

Notes from Patti:

A food processor can be used to make the dough. Insert a chopping blade, add all ingredients at the same time and using the on/off method, process until dough forms a ball.

Rotate after 15 minutes. Be sure to time the drying period or the dough will become overdried. Fold it over and over into a roll about 3" wide. Slice into noodles. After cutting the noodles, open them on a clean, dry cloth and allow to dry at least another 15 minutes. If using a pasta machine, follow the manufacturer's instructions.

You cannot use too much water to cook pasta–at least 6 quarts per pound. Bring water to a rolling boil, add 1 tablespoon salt, 2 tablespoons oil and the pasta. Cook about 5 minutes or until "al dente", which means tender but still slightly resistant to the bite. The more you make pasta the easier it becomes, so practice, practice, practice! Makes 1 pound, enough to serve 4.

Peppered Pasta

4 large bell peppers, 2 green and 2 red, stemmed,
 seeded and rib removed, cut into strips
1/3 cup olive oil
1 large onion, thinly sliced
2 lbs. ripe tomatoes, peeled, seeded and coarsely
 chopped
2/3 cup minced fresh basil leaves
1/3 hot red pepper, seeded and minced
Salt and freshly ground black pepper to taste
2 Tbsps. capers, drained and rinsed
1/2 cup Zinfandel

Notes from Patti:

To prevent freshly made pasta from sticking together sprinkle RICE FLOUR between layers. Wrap in plastic wrap and refrigerate. Can be kept for several days. Rice flour can be found in most supermarkets in the ethnic food department.

In a large heavy skillet, heat oil until haze forms. Add onions and saute until transparent. Add peppers. Cook over high heat for 5 minutes, stirring constantly. Add tomatoes, basil, hot pepper and season with salt and pepper. Add Zinfandel. Reduce heat and simmer 10 minutes. Serve over fresh egg noodles. Garnish with capers. Serves 4. Pinot Noir may be substituted for the Zinfandel.

Pasta Ala Predika

This recipe was created to honor my long time, dear friend Jerry Predika. Jerry is the author of the "The Sausage Making Cookbook", the most complete work I've seen on the subject. He teaches sausage making and wine appreciation and is currently writing a book on wine.

Notes from Patti:

Because Jerry eats a lot of highly seasoned food accompanied by very hot peppers, his friends say he won't have to go to hell to find out how hot it is — his mouth already knows! When I make this dish for him I always add several pinches of red pepper flakes the last 20 minutes of cooking time. This is hot but not too hot to handle if your family likes a bit of heat.

2 lbs. hot Italian sausage links, preferably homemade
2 cups sweet style Johannisberg Riesling
3 Tbsps. olive oil
2 Tbsps. butter
2 medium white onions, coarsely chopped
2 red bell peppers, stemmed seeds and ribs removed,
*   Cut into strips.*
2 cups Cabernet Sauvignon
1–2 lb. can Italian plum tomatoes, with liquid
1 Tbsp. dried oregano
1 tsp. thyme
Salt and pepper to taste
1/2 cup coarsely chopped parsley
10 large cloves garlic, minced
1 lb. mostaccioli
8 Tbsps. freshly grated Parmesan cheese

Prick sausage links on both sides with the tines of a fork. Pour Johannisberg Riesling into heavy dutch oven and add the sausage. Place the pot, uncovered, in a 375°F oven for 30 minutes. Remove from oven, turn the links and return to the oven for another 30 minutes or until well browned. Remove links from pot and drain on paper toweling. Pour any fat out of the pot. Set in oven at low heat and add the olive oil and butter. Add onions and cook until transparent, about 10 minutes; add pepper and cook until tender, stirring occasionally. Add Cabernet Sauvignon, tomatoes, oregano, thyme, salt and pepper to taste and bring to a boil. Reduce heat and simmer, covered for 30 minutes. Slice the sausage into 1/2" pieces. Add sausage to sauce and continue to simmer, uncovered, another 20 to 30 minutes, stirring occasionally. Stir in parsley and garlic, adjust seasoning if necessary, and simmer another 10 minutes. Meanwhile, bring 6 quarts salted water to a full rolling boil. Add mostaccioli, a little at a time and bring back to the boil. Cook 5 minutes or until tender but firm. Drain pasta and pour into large bowl. Add sauce and toss. Top each serving with 1 tablespoon cheese. Serves 8. A sweet style Gewurztraminer may be substituted for the Cabernet Sauvignon.

Manicotti with Marinara Sauce

I never get enough of this sauce because it must be made with vine ripened tomatoes and fresh basil. It can be made with canned tomatoes but it isn't as good.

Marinara Sauce

3 Tbsps. olive oil
1 small white onion, diced
6 cloves garlic, minced
3 1/2 to 4 lbs. vine ripened tomatoes, peeled, seeded and
*   coarsely chopped*
20 to 25 fresh basil leaves, chopped
2 tsps. fresh thyme, minced
4 Tbsps. fresh Italian parsley, chopped
Salt and pepper to taste
1/2 cup Merlot

In a large heavy saucepan heat oil until a haze forms. Add onions and garlic and saute until onion is transparent. Add tomatoes, basil thyme and parsley and simmer 10 minutes. Season with salt and pepper, add Merlot and simmer additional 5 to 10 minutes until sauce thickens. Pinot Noir may be substituted for Merlot.

8 uncooked manicotti shells
3/4 lb. lean ground beef
1 medium white onion, minced
2 Tbsps. olive oil
1 cup soft bread crumbs
1–10 oz. pkg. frozen spinach
1/4 cup Parmesan cheese
3 eggs slightly beaten
Salt and pepper to taste

Brown meat and onions in oil until onions are transparent. Set aside. Thaw spinach completely and place in a terry cloth towel and twist until all liquid is removed. Remove spinach to mixing bowl. Add bread crumbs, cheese and eggs and blend. Fold in browned beef and onions. Cover bottom of a 2 quart baking dish with one cup marinara sauce. Fill UNCOOKED manicotti shells with meat mixture, arrange stuffed shells in a single layer in baking dish, leaving space between each shell to allow for expansion. Cover shells with remaining sauce. Cover baking dish with aluminum foil. Bake in a preheated 375°F oven for one hour. Serves 4.

Zita with Fresh Vegetables

Zita is a rice shaped pasta most often used in soups, but I have used it for years as a side dish and any vegetables you like, such as broccoli, mushrooms and snow peas.

Notes from Patti:

The way to peel tomatoes is to dip them in boiling water for 15 to 20 seconds. Remove with slotted spoon and skins will slip off easily.

4 quarts boiling salted water
1–16 oz. package zita pasta
3 Tbsps. olive oil
3 Tbsps. butter
6 fresh green onions with 1' of green stems, sliced
1 large clove garlic, minced
1 green bell pepper, stemmed, seeded and ribs removed,
   coarsely chopped
2 large tomatoes, peeled, seeded and coarsely chopped
Salt and coarsely ground black pepper to taste
2 Tbsp. minced parsley

Add zita to boiling water and cook 8 to 10 minutes until pasta is firm but tender. Drain in a wire mesh sieve and set aside. In a large heavy skillet, heat oil until haze forms. Add butter, onions, garlic and bell pepper. Saute over medium heat until peppers are tender, about 5 minutes. Add zita and toss. Add tomatoes and toss. Season with salt and pepper. Add parsley and toss again. Serves 8 generously.

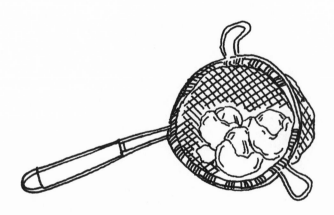

Pasta with Summer Vegetables

This is one of my favorite summer dishes. You can use any fresh vegetables in almost any combination. Not only is this delicious, it looks marvelous!

2 Tbsps. good olive oil
2 Tbsps. butter
2 cloves garlic, crushed
1/4 cup dry vermouth
2 medium size zucchini, sliced
1/2 medium onion, diced
1 green bell pepper, cored and diced
1 red bell pepper, cored and diced
1 small hot pepper, cored and diced
2 medium tomatoes, cored, seeded and diced
Salt and pepper to taste
1/2 lb. fresh egg pasta

In a large heavy skillet, heat olive oil. Add butter and melt. Add garlic and stir until slightly browned. Add vermouth and simmer until alcohol burns off. Remove garlic and discard. Add all vegetables except tomatoes. Saute for 3 to 4 minutes. Season with salt and pepper. In a large pot, bring 4 quarts of water to a rolling boil. Add pasta and stir until water returns to a rolling boil. Drain and set aside. Add tomatoes to other vegetables in skillet and toss only until tomatoes are heated through. Add pasta to vegetables and toss until well mixed. Serve at once. Serves 4.

Lasagne Roll Ups

My grandma made this dish often but she used marinara sauce. I sometimes make it that way but I love the look and flavor of the pesto sauce.

1 lb. lasagne noodles
2 Tbsps. olive oil
1 lb. ricotta cheese
2 cups freshly grated Parmesan cheese
1 cup finely minced mozzarella cheese
2 Tbsps. dry sherry
1/2 cup minced fresh Italian parsley
3 fresh green onions, white part only, minced
1 large egg yolk
4 large cloves garlic, minced
1/2 tsp. dried basil
1/2 tsp. marjoram
1/4 tsp. oregano
Salt and freshly ground black pepper
1 recipe A DIFFERENT PESTO SAUCE

Cook lasagne in 8 quarts boiling salted water until tender but firm. About 6 to 8 minutes. Drain and gently toss with oil. Place on paper toweling and set aside. In a large bowl, combine cheeses with sherry. Blend in egg yolk and garlic. Add basil, marjoram and oregano. Season with salt and pepper. Generously butter a 2 1/2 quart baking dish. Spread portion of cheese sauce over each noodle. Roll each noodle, jelly roll fashion and stand vertically in single layer in baking dish. Spoon pesto sauce over each noodle. Bake in preheated 350°F oven for 30 minutes. Serves 6. No substitute for dry sherry.

Tagliatelle with Gorgonzola Sauce

TAGLIATELLE is a flat egg noodle about twice as wide as fettucini noodles and best used with cream sauces.

2 Tbsps. butter
2 large cloves garlic cloves minced
1/2 cup Gorgonzola cheese, crumbled
1/3 cup milk
1/4 cup heavy cream
1 lb. tagliatelle noodles

Melt butter in heavy skillet and saute garlic until barely browned. Add milk. Place over low flame. Mash the Gorgonzola with a wooden spoon and stir to incoporate it into the milk and butter. Cook until the sauce has a dense creamy consistency. Set aside. Cook the tagliatelle until al dente, drain. Return sauce to low flame and stir in cream. Toss pasta with sauce. Serves 6.

Notes from Patti:

Look for gorgonzola that is white in color and soft to the touch. I have substituted blue cheese, but I have never achieved the texture and flavor of this sauce with any cheese but choice imported gorgonzola

Fresh Pasta with Gorgonzola Sauce

1 1/2 cups dry vermouth
2 cups heavy cream
Freshly ground black pepper to taste
1/8 tsp. freshly grated nutmeg
1/2 lb. Gorgonzola cheese, crumbled
2 Tbsps. freshly grated Parmesan cheese
6 quarts boiling salted water
1 lb. fresh egg noodles

Pour vermouth in a small heavy saucepan and bring to a boil. Reduce by half. Add cream, bring to a boil and lower heat to a simmer. Season with pepper and nutmeg. Remove sauce from heat and add Gorgonzola cheese. Stir until cheese is incorporated. Stir in parmesan. Cover and set aside. Add fresh pasta to 6 quarts of boiling salted water and cook, stirring constantly until water returns to a boil. Boil 1/2 to 1minute, remove from heat and drain. Transfer pasta to a heated platter. Stir sauce and pour over pasta, toss and serve immediately. Serves 4. No substitute for the dry vermouth.

Spaghetti with Mock Pesto

Notes from Patti:

This is truly low calorie without tasting that way. The nuts provide good protein and since oil and cheese are not used you can eat a lot and not feel guilty!

1 lb. spaghetti
1/4 cup walnuts
4 large cloves garlic, halved
1 cup large curd cottage cheese
3 cups fresh basil leaves, tightly packed
2 fresh green onions, white part only
Salt and pepper to taste

Put walnuts and garlic in food processor fitted with a steel blade. Process until finely chopped. Add remaining ingredients and process until smooth, scraping down the sides of bowl as needed. Cook spaghetti until tender but firm, drain and toss with sauce. Serves 6.

No Cook Tomato-Basil Sauce with Fettucini

2 lbs. Italian plum tomatoes, halved, seeded and
 cut into thin strips
1 large green bell pepper, stemmed, seeded, ribs
 removed and cut into thin strips
1 cup chopped fresh basil
3 large cloves garlic, minced
2/3 cup olive oil
3 Tbsps. cream sherry
Salt and freshly ground pepper to taste
1/2 lb. mozzarella cheese, cut in 1/2" cubes, set aside
12 black pitted olives, sliced, set aside
1 lb. fresh fettucini
1/4 cup freshly grated Parmesan cheese

In a large bowl, combine tomatoes, peppers, basil and garlic. Stir cream sherry into oil and pour over tomato mixture. Cover and refrigerate for several hours. Before serving, bring mixture to room temperature. Bring 4 quarts salted water to a boil. Add fettucini and bring back to boil. Cook 2 to 3 minutes until tender but firm. Drain and toss with tomato mixture. Add salt and pepper to taste, mozzarella and olives and toss. Sprinkle with Parmesan cheese. Serves 6. No substitute for cream sherry.

My Favorite Spaghetti Sauce

Sugar is often used in tomato sauces to counteract the acid. I learned to use cream sherry from Grandma. The flavor will surprise you.

1 large white onion, coarsely chopped
1/3 cup olive oil
1 celery rib, finely chopped
3 large cloves garlic, minced
1–8 oz. can Italian plum tomatoes, broken in pieces
1–8 oz. can tomato sauce
3 Tbsp. tomato paste
1 1/2 cups Merlot
3 Tbsp. cream sherry
2 Tbsps. minced parsley
1/2 tsp. oregano
1 tsp. basil
Salt and freshly ground pepper to taste

In a large stockpot, heat olive oil until haze forms. Add onion, celery and garlic and saute until celery is tender, about 5 minutes. Add tomatoes, tomato sauce and tomato paste and stir. Bring to a boil. Add Merlot and cream sherry and stir. Add parsley, oregano and basil. Season with salt and pepper. Cover, lower heat and simmer 45 minutes. Makes about 3 pints. Pinot Noir may be substituted for Merlot. No substitute for cream sherry.

Linguine with Clam Sauce

1 cup olive oil
8 large cloves garlic, minced
4 dozen raw clams, shucked and chopped coarsely,
    all liquor reserved
2 1/2 cups clam juice
1/2 cup dry vermouth
1/2 cup finely minced parsley
2 tsps. dried oregano
Salt and coarsely ground black pepper to taste
6 quarts boiling salted water
1 lb. linguine

Heat oil in a heavy dutch oven. Add garlic and cook in oven at low heat until brown, about 3 to 4 minutes. Combine reserved clam liquor and clam juice. Add juices, dry vermouth, parsley, oregano, salt and pepper to the dutch oven. Simmer, partially covered for 10 minutes. Add linguine to boiling salted water and cook al dente (tender but firm.). Drain and add to clam sauce. Toss thoroughly and serve in soup bowls. Serve with lots of hot garlic bread. Serves 4 hungry people or 6 not so hungry. No substitute for dry vermouth.

Fried Pasta

Notes from Patti:

You can fry any style of left over pasta as long as you remove as much liquid as possible. This is a wonderful way to use left over vegetables, small amounts of meats or fowl. A few chopped black olives add wonderful flavor. A teflon coated skillet is probably the best choice, since the pasta will not stick to the surface.

There is no real recipe for FRIED PASTA, but it has been around as long as the noodle itself. I am told FRIED PASTA is Neapolitan in origin, but there is no area of Italy that doesn't have their own version of this dish. I've had it with a simple cheese and parsley dressing to an elegant asparagus and cream dressing. In the United States, the most common version is fried left over spaghetti–wonderful for brunch.

> *1 lb. pasta, such as spaghetti or macaroni, cooked*
> *   al dente*
> *1/2 cup freshly grated parmesan cheese*
> *1/4 cup minced parsley*
> *2 Tbsps. butter, melted*
> *2 large eggs beaten*
> *Salt and freshly ground black pepper to taste*
> *Oil for frying*

Toss cooked pasta with cheese, parsley and melted butter. Add beaten eggs, a little at a time, tossing each time. Season with salt and pepper to taste. Heat oil in a large heavy skillet. Drop heaping tablespoons of mixture in hot oil. Fry until deep brown, turn and brown other side. Serve piping hot with more cheese.

Lemon Pilaf

> *2 Tbsps. butter*
> *1/2 cup onion, finely minced*
> *1 cup long grain white rice*
> *1 1/2 cup chicken stock*
> *1/2 cup dry sherry*
> *1/4 cup lemon juice*
> *Zest of 1 lemon, finely minced*
> *3 Tbsps. white raisins*
> *1/4 cup toasted, slivered almonds*

In a large saucepan, melt 1 tablespoon of the butter. Add onions and saute just until onions are soft. Add rice and stir until all the grains are coated with butter. Stir in chicken stock, dry sherry, lemon juice, zest and white raisins. Lower heat and cover. Simmer until liquid is absorbed, about 20 minutes. Stir in remaining butter and almonds and serve at once. Serves 4. There is no substitute for dry sherry.

Patti's Pasta Primavera

1 lb. cappellini (very thin spaghetti)
1 bunch broccoli, trimmed and cut into flowerettes,
   peel stems and cut into julienne strips
2 large carrots, pared and sliced
2 medium zucchini, sliced
1 sweet red bell, pepper, cored, seeded
   and cut into julienne strips
3 Tbsps. olive oil
2 Tbsps. butter
1 large clove garlic, mashed
1/2 cup freshly grated Parmesan cheese

Notes from Patti:

You may use any com-
bination of vegetables you
like, as long as they are
fresh.

Steam broccoli flowerettes, stems and carrots until tender-crisp.
Set aside. Saute zucchini and sweet pepper in 1 tablespoon oil until
tender-crisp. Set aside. Cook cappellini al dente and drain. In a
large heavy skillet, heat remaining olive oil and butter until a haze
forms. Add garlic. Turn off heat and toss pasta in oil mixture.
Add vegetables and toss well. Serve at once with freshly grated
Parmesan cheese. Serves 6.

Pasta with Broccoli

1 bunch fresh broccoli
1/2 cup boiling water
1/2 tsp. salt
8 oz. large pasta twists
1 Tbsp. olive oil
1 Tbsp. butter
2 cloves garlic, crushed
1/2 tsp. dried basil
1/2 cup chicken stock
1/4 cup parsley, finely chopped
4 Tbsps. freshly grated Parmesan cheese
1/4 tsp. pepper
1 cup cottage cheese

Wash and remove leaves from broccoli. Remove flowerettes.
Split each stalk lengthwise into halves and chop. Arrange stalks
and flowerettes in bottom of a large skillet. Pour boiling water over
broccoli and sprinkle with salt. Cook, covered, over medium heat
about 8 minutes or until water is evaporated. Cook pasta in boiling
water until al dente (firm to the tooth) and drain well. Heat olive oil
and butter in a large skillet. Saute garlic and basil until garlic is
tender. Add chicken stock, parsley, Parmesan cheese, pepper and
broccoli. Stir until well blended. Remove from heat and stir in
cottage cheese. Toss broccoli mixture with pasta and serve at once.
Serves 6.

Spinach Fettuccini Timbales

1 3/4 cups freshly grated Parmesan cheese
1 1/4 cups cream fraiche
1 1/4 cups ricotta cheese
1 1/4 cups half and half
4 large eggs
2 tsps. salt
1/2 tsp. freshly ground pepper
1 cup fresh basil leaves, minced
1 lb. fresh spinach fettucini, cooked al dente

Notes from Patti:

I'm always looking for "do ahead" dishes and these little beauties can be made and frozen up to two weeks ahead.

Generously butter 3 non-stick muffin pans. Sprinkle 1 teaspoon Parmesan cheese into each cup, tilting pan to distribute evenly. Blend1/2 cup Parmesan, cream fraiche, ricotta, half and half, eggs, salt and pepper in food processor. Process until smooth. Blend in basil. Measure 2 tablespoons mixture into each cup. Mound pasta in cups. Pour remaining mixture into cups, filing almost to the top. Sprinkle 1 teaspoon Parmesan cheese over each cup. Freeze until firm, at least 2 hours. Cover with foil and return to freezer. Position rack on lower part of oven and preheat to 375°F. Bake frozen timbales uncovered until bottoms are browned, about 35 minutes. Loosen with a sharp knife and serve hot.

San Francisco Fettucini

I was served this wonderful dish at the California Culinary Academy and they kindly gave me the recipe.

1 Tbsp. butter
2 shallots, finely chopped
1 cup Sauvignon Blanc
1 quart heavy cream
4 large cloves garlic, finely minced
4 oz. Roquefort cheese
4 oz. freshly grated parmesan cheese
Salt and pepper to taste
1/4 tsp. nutmeg
4 tsp. butter, cut into small pieces and allowed
 to soften to room temperature
1 large egg yolk
1 1/2 lbs. fresh fettucini

In a large skillet, saute shallots in butter until they are translucent. Add Sauvignon Blanc and simmer until liquid is reduced to about 1/4 cup. Add cream and reduce by 1/3. being careful not to boil. Add garlic, cheeses and seasonings. remove from heat and whisk in butter and egg yolk. Cook the fettucini in 1 1/2 gallons boiling salted water, just until pasta is al dente, (firm to the bite.) Drain and toss with sauce. Garnish with fresh chopped basil and serve with extra parmesan cheese. Serves 6. Fume Blanc may be substituted for Sauvignon Blanc.

Tagliarini with Sherry Walnut Sauce

6 quarts boiling salted water
12 oz. tagliarini
2 cups walnuts
4 cloves garlic
2 Tbsps. dry sherry
2 Tbsps. butter
1/4 cup olive oil
3/4 cup freshly grated Parmesan cheese

Cook pasta in boiling water until tender but firm, about 10 minutes. Meanwhile, put walnuts, garlic, and sherry in the bowl of a food processor fitted with a steel blade and process until smooth. Add butter, oil and cheese and continue to process until smooth. Add a bit more sherry if sauce is too thick. Drain pasta and transfer to a platter and add sauce. Toss and serve immediately. Serves 4. No substitute for dry sherry.

Seafood

Grandpa loved to fish only a little better than Grandma loved his catch. I don't think it occurred to him to come home without fish because Grandma had planned on them for the evening meal. If Grandpa wasn't fishing, one of his friends was and there was always plenty for everyone. I was well into my teens before I realized people actually paid money for fish.

During clamming season, entire families, aunts, uncles, cousins, grandparents and anyone else who wanted to come along went to the shore to dig for clams. We would build huge bonfires and scrub the clams in the ocean and steam them right on the beach. There was always fresh sourdough bread to dip in the pot and wine to drink with the clams. Everyone would eat until there wasn't a clam left.

My own husband was a stream fisherman and tried to introduce me to this skill, without much luck. But we came to a happy conclusion--while he fished, I would walk the steam in search of wild greens, onions and sometimes I would find edible mushrooms. We would build a fire and stuff the fish with my find and cook them over the coals. I have never eaten any food as delicious, nor have I been able to create those heavenly flavors in my own kitchen.

I wish you the pleasure of the great gifts our oceans and streams offer up to us.

Seafood and Pasta Extravaganza

Webster's dictionary defines the word extravaganza as "a lavish or spectacular show or event". This dish is certainly spectacular and will make any gathering an event. Since marinating is involved, this dish is best prepared in three stages.

Day One:
1 1/2 cups olive oil
3/4 cup white wine vinegar
4 large cloves garlic, minced as fine as possible
1 Tbsp. dry mustard
1/2 tsp. dry rosemary
1 tsp. dill weed

In a jar with a tight fitting lid, combine oil, vinegar, garlic, mustard, rosemary and dill weed. Cover and thoroughly shake. Set aside.

1 lb. fresh egg noodles
1 lb. fresh spinach noodles
1 lb. fresh tomato noodles

Bring 6 quarts of salted water to a full rolling boil. Add egg noodles and bring back to boil. Cook 30 seconds, stirring constantly. Check a strand between fingers. It should be tender but firm. Drain and pour into a large bowl. Shake marinade and divide into 3 equal parts. Pour 1 part over noodles and toss. Cool to room temperature and transfer to a large plastic bag. Refrigerate. Repeat steps with spinach and tomato noodles.

Day Two:
1/2 cup olive oil
1/4 cup white wine vinegar
1 tsp. dry mustard
1 tsp. salt

In a jar with a tight fitting lid, combine oil, vinegar, mustard and salt Cover and thoroughly shake. Set aside.

1 large bunch broccoli, cut into flowerettes
1 head cauliflower, cut into flowerettes
6 fresh green onions, white part only, sliced
1 lb. fresh mushrooms, sliced

Steam broccoli and cauliflower just until tender-crisp. Cool to room temperature. In a large bowl toss broccoli, cauliflower, onions and mushrooms with marinade. Cover and refrigerate.

3/4 cup olive oil
1/4 cup Champagne vinegar
1/4 cup lemon juice
1/2 tsp. dill weed
2 lbs. medium size raw shrimp, shelled and deveined
1 lb. scallops

In a jar with a tight fitting lid, combine oil, vinegar, lemon juice and dill weed. Cover and thoroughly shake. Set aside. Steam shrimp just until pink. Steam scallops til barely tender. Cool to room temperature. In a large bowl toss shrimp and scallops with marinade, cover and refrigerate.

Day Three:
1 package frozen baby peas, thawed
1 pint cherry tomatoes, washed, and stemmed

You will need a large round platter, about 25-30" across the widest point. If you don't own one this size, try your local rental store. Drain the tomato noodles and arrange around the outer rim of the platter. Drain the egg noodles and arrange next to the tomato noodles. Next, drain the spinach noodles and arrange next to the egg noodles, leaving a well in the center of the platter. Drain the vegetables and seafood and toss together. Fill the well with the vegetables and seafood mixture. Arrange cherry tomatoes on top of the egg noodles and sprinkle the baby peas overall. Cover with plastic wrap and refrigerate until serving time. Serves 15-20 for a fantastic party!

Pesto-Stuffed Sea Scallops

1 cup pesto
1 1/2 lbs. large sea scallops (about 30 scallops)
3/4 cup Chardonnay
1/4 cup olive oil

Cut deep slit across top of each scallop with a sharp knife, without cutting through the bottom. Place scallops in large bowl and pour Chardonnay over scallops. Cover and refrigerate 1 hour. Drain scallops and pat dry with paper toweling. Fit pastry bag with small plain tip. Spoon pesto into bag. Pipe pesto into each scallop. Place broiler pan 3 inches from source of heat. Preheat broiler. Place scallops on heated broiler pan and brush with olive oil. Broil 5 to 6 minutes, just until opaque and cooked through.

Grandma's Mustard Shrimp

Notes from Patti:

This has been a family favorite for many years and it couldn't be easier to prepare. I use it often as an antipasto dish but when shrimp were more affordable I made great platters of this dish for Saturday night suppers. But my favorite way to serve this dish is still Sunday brunch; just prepare it the night before and pop it into the oven just before serving. Wonderful!

Grandmother use to crush mustard seeds and add them to prepared mustard for this dish–today I use a Dijon or German style mustard.

24 large shrimp, shelled (leaving tail) and deveined
3 Tbsps. olive oil
2 Tbsps. butter, softened
1 Tbsp. lemon juice
1/4 cup dry vermouth
2 Tbsps. Dijon style mustard
1 tsp. soy sauce
6 large cloves garlic, minced

Place shrimp in a single layer in shallow baking dish. Combine all remaining ingredients and blend thoroughly. Pour over shrimp, cover and refrigerate at least 2 hours–longer is better. Broil in preheated oven 5 minutes.

Dilled Shrimp

This dish is a beauty because it can be served in many different ways. It's wonderful as an antipasto dish served with pickled peppers; as a delightful hors d'oeuvre for cocktail hour. These shrimp make a great salad served on a bed of bibb lettuce.

20 large shrimp in shells
1/3 cup lemon juice
1/3 cup olive oil
2 Tbsps. white wine vinegar
3 Tbsps. fresh dill, chopped
2 Tbsps. parsley, chopped, without stems
2 cloves garlic, finely minced
1 medium red onion, sliced and separated into rings

Bring a large pot of water to a boil. Add 1 teaspoon salt and a large piece of lemon. Add shrimp, stir and bring back to a boil. Drain and remove shells. Shrimp should be pink and firm. Toss shrimp with remaining ingredients. Cover and refrigerate several hours before serving. Serves 8 as antipasto or 4 as a salad.

Cheese Shrimp Fritters

2 cups shredded Gouda cheese
3 Tbsps. all-purpose flour
1 tsp. baking soda
1/2 small white onion, finely minced
3/4 tsp. dill weed
3 Tbsps. dry sherry
2 large eggs, well beaten
1 cup chopped, cooked shrimp
Corn oil for deep frying

Mix cheese, flour, baking soda, onion and dill weed in a large bowl. Stir dry sherry into eggs. Add egg mixture and mix until cheese is evenly distributed. Stir in shrimp. Heat oil to 370°F. Carefully drop teaspoons of batter into the oil. Cook until fritters are golden brown, about three minutes, turning once during the cooking period. Drain on paper toweling. Serve hot or cold. Makes 3 dozen.

Notes from Patti:

These little fritters are wonderful for the antipasto course and I love them for lunch served with a big green salad. They also freeze very well.

Shrimp in Riesling/Dijon Sauce

"This is sinful! Particularly nice for a romantic dinner for two–no "black tie". Throw caution and Emily Post to the wind and enjoy dipping the bread in the wonderful sauce."–Jill

3 Tbsps. olive oil
3 Tbsps. butter
4 large cloves of garlic, cut in half lengthwise
1 cup medium-dry White Riesling
2 Tbsps. Dijon style mustard
2 lbs. shrimp, shelled and deveined

In a large, heavy skillet heat oil and butter until a haze forms. Add garlic and cook until browned. Remove garlic and discard. Add wine and bring to a boil. Lower heat and whisk in mustard. Add shrimp and cook until shrimp are pink (3 to 4 minutes). Serve with lots of sourdough bread for dunking in the sauce and, of course, drink the rest of the Riesling with the shrimp.

Michael's Grilled Salmon Steaks

My son Michael has always been a decent cook but in the last few years he has learned to trust his instincts and has become adventuresome in the kitchen. So much so, his wife and daughters welcome him in the kitchen–and you're always welcome in my kitchen sweetie!

1/4 cup butter
1/4 cup Gewurztraminer
1/2 tsp. dill weed
2 fresh green onions, sliced with part of greens
2 large cloves garlic, finely minced
Peel from 1 lemon, coarsely chopped
1/4 tsp. coarsely ground black pepper
1/4 cup fresh lemon juice
4 large salmon steaks, 1" thick

Melt butter and combine with all remaining ingredients, except salmon. Whisk until thoroughly blended. Place salmon steaks in a shallow glass baking dish and cover with marinade. Turn once, being sure salmon is completely coated with marinade. Allow steaks to marinate 1/2 hour to 45 minutes. Prepare barbecue coals by igniting about 25 briquets. When coals are covered with gray ash, spread in a single layer. Oil grill thoroughly. Set grill 4 to 6 inches above coals. Place steaks on grill and cook NOT MORE THAN 4 MINUTES OF EACH SIDE. Basting often. Serves 4. An off dry White Riesling may be substituted for Gewurztraminer.

Halibut Almondine

This is the perfect dish when you want something really good but have little time to cook. A simple green salad, sourdough bread and the rest of the bottle of Riesling make a perfect dinner.

1 lb. halibut fillets
1/2 tsp. salt
4 Tbsps. butter
4 Tbsps. slivered almonds
1/2 cup dry style Johannisberg Riesling
1 Tbsp. fresh lemon juice
1 lemon cut into 4 wedges

Sprinkle fish with salt. Melt butter in skillet and brown fillets on both sides, not more than 3 to 4 minutes on each side. Transfer to a warm platter. Add almonds to pan drippings and brown. Add Johannisberg Riesling and bring to a boil. Cook until Riesling is reduced to half. Stir in lemon juice. Pour sauce over fillets and garnish with lemon wedges. Serves 4. Sauvignon Blanc may be substituted for the Johannisberg Riesling but the dry style of Riesling lends a more subtle flavor.

Red Snapper with Lemon Butter

Lemons are a great enhancer for almost all seafood, but particularly lends its flavor to baked or broiled fish fillets.

> *1 cube butter at room temperature*
> *2 Tbsps. lemon juice*
> *2 Tbsps. parsley, minced*
> *2 Tbsps. chives, minced*
> *2 Tbsps. scallions, minced*
> *1/2 tsp. dill weed*
> *3 lemons, cut in 1/4" slices*
> *1 1/2 to 2 lbs. red snapper fillets*
> *1/2 cup Chardonnay*

Combine butter, lemon juice, parsley, chives, scallions, and dill weed in a small bowl. Whisk with wire whip until well blended and fluffy. Shape into a cylinder, freezer wrap and freeze. Line a shallow ovenproof dish with a layer of lemon slices. Lay red snapper fillet to fit snugly in a single layer over lemon slices. Pour Chardonnay over fillets. Place a 2" slice of lemon butter on each fillet. Bake in a preheated 350°F oven, uncovered, for 12 to 15 minutes, depending on thickness of fillets. Serves 4. Sauvignon Blanc may be substituted for Chardonnay.

Notes from Patti:

Not only is this lemon butter wonderful with all kinds of fish, it's wonderful with fork-tender vegetables such as broccoli, green beans and a very different flavor for carrots.

Striped Bass
with Garlic and Pecan Sauce

My mother and father didn't think much about food; they truly ate to live, unlike the rest of the family. But when mama (Grandma) made this dish, my mother always seemed to enjoy it very much. It remains among our family's favorite seafood dishes.

> *2 large egg yolks*
> *2 Tbsps. white wine vinegar*
> *1 Tbsp. fresh lemon juice*
> *2 large cloves garlic (I like more)*
> *1 cup plus 2 tablespoons olive oil*
> *Salt and freshly ground pepper to taste*
> *1/2 cup coarsely ground pecans*
> *1/2 cup minced fresh parsley*
> *6 skinless fillets of striped bass,*
> *about 8 to 10 ounces each*

Place eggs, vinegar, lemon juice and garlic in a food processor fitted with a steel blade and process until smooth. With the motor running, gradually pour, in a steady stream, 1 cup olive oil. Process until all the oil is incorporated and sauce thickens. Pour into a small bowl, scraping sides of processor bowl. Season with salt and pepper and whisk in pecans and parsley. Set aside. Preheat broiler. Brush the fillets on both sides with remaining 2 tbsps. oil. Broil 4 inches from the source of heat, without turning, for 4 to 5 minutes or until fish flakes easily. Transfer fillets to heated platter and spoon sauce evenly over the fish. Garnish with lemon slices. Serves 6.

Steamed Mussels
with Chardonnay and Shallots

Notes from Patti:

You must have plenty of fresh, crusty sourdough bread to sop up this wonderful sauce…

4 lbs. mussels, cleaned and debearded
3 Tbsps. shallots, chopped
2 Tbsps. parsley, chopped
3/4 cup Chardonnay
Juice of 1/2 lemon
Freshly ground black pepper to taste

Combine all ingredients in a large heavy saucepan with a lid and bring to a boil. Steam until mussels open, about 4-5 minutes. Serve immediately. Serves 4. Sauvignon Blanc may be substituted for the Chardonnay but I much prefer the Chardonnay, after all, the bottle is open so pour and enjoy the wine with your friends!

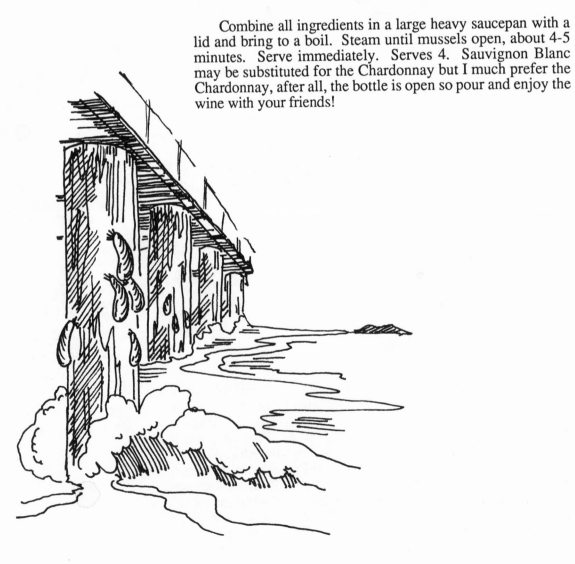

Seafood Au Gratin

1 lb. shrimp, cooked
1/2 lb. crab, cooked
1/2 lb. lobster, cooked
2 Tbsps. butter
2 Tbsps. flour
1/2 cup Chardonnay
1/2 cup chicken stock
1/2 cup heavy cream
1 tsp. Worcestershire sauce
2 dashes Tabasco
1 tsp. fresh green onion, finely minced
Salt and pepper to taste
Juice from 1/2 lemon
1 cup bread crumbs
1/2 cup Gruyere cheese, freshly grated
3 Tbsps. butter, melted

Cut shellfish into bite size pieces and set aside. Place butter and flour in a medium size heavy saucepan. Cook, stirring constantly until butter and flour are well blended. Add Chardonnay, chicken stock and heavy cream and continue cooking until well blended. Add worcestershire sauce, tabasco, onion, salt and pepper to taste and lemon juice. Whisk in shellfish. Butter six individual au gratin dishes or large clam shells. Divide mixture between the dishes. Top with bread crumbs, cheese and melted butter. Bake in a preheated 425°F oven for 20 minutes or until nicely browned. Serves 6.

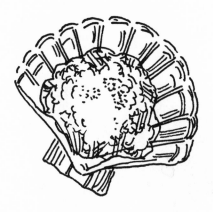

Marinated Calamari

Notes from Patti:

The lemon juice "cooks" the squid and leaves it "chewy" in texture. If the idea of raw squid bothers you, simply steam until tender and proceed with the recipe. This dish is so good you will soon be asked to make more and more of it. You can buy squid, already cleaned, in 4 1/2 to 5 pound frozen blocks. Set the block in your sink and cover with cold water for a half an hour to defrost. Simply double all other ingredients and you have the makings for a great party!

Marinated Calamari is good any time, but my favorite time for this dish is November and December when we give and go to so many parties. It's delicious, easy to prepare and somehow unexpected this time of year.

> *2 lbs. squid, cleaned and cut into bite size pieces*
> *1/2 cup lemon juice*
> *1/2 cup Chardonnay*
> *1 1/2 heads garlic, peeled and chopped very fine*
> *1/2 bunch parsley without stems, chopped fine*
> *1/2 tsp. dill weed*
> *1/2 tsp. cracked black pepper*
> *1/2 cup good virgin olive oil*
> *2 Tbsps. red wine vinegar*

In a large bowl, combine squid and lemon juice. Set aside for one hour. Add Chardonnay and mix well. Combine remaining ingredients and pour over squid. Stir well. Cover and refrigerate at least 24 hours (48 hours even better). Serve with hot crusty sourdough bread and the rest of the Chardonnay. Serves 8 to 10. Sauvignon Blanc may be substituted for the Chardonnay.

Cynthia's Ceviche

Cynthia Kaiser is a wonderfully gifted young women. She graduated with top honors from the oldest and most prestigious hotel school in Vienna, Austria. She has owned her own bakery and is currently the executive chef at the elegant La Playa Hotel in Carmel, California.

> *Juice and zest of 2 fresh limes*
> *Juice and zest of 1 orange*
> *Juice and zest of 1 lemon*
> *1 Tbsp. white wine vinegar*
> *1/2 tsp. Kosher Salt*
> *White pepper to taste*
> *1/2 lb scallops, thinly sliced*
> *1/2 pound salmon fillet, cut into 1/2" cubes*
> *1/2 cup fresh chopped chives*

Combine citrus juices and wine vinegar in a glass bowl; add salt, pepper, and citrus zest. Whisk until well blended. Add scallops and salmon. Toss until well coated. Refrigerate 2 to 4 hours. Garnish with chives.

Poultry

"The rooster may look fancy but the hen can lay an egg". I have no idea where this old adage comes from but I've heard it all my life. Be it rooster or hen, the noble fowl is as old as history and known to exist in every part of the world. Chickens are celebrated in literature, art, music, folklore and they provide us with a never ending supply of food. I have been with chickens all of my life and have collected them, in one form or another for years.

There is almost no cuisine that doesn't include chickens and their incredible edible by-product, the egg. The versatility of poultry as a food is astounding. It can be baked, broiled, stuffed, sauteed, stewed, fried and on and on. Is there one among us who doesn't believe chicken soup will make us feel better when we are ill? I can remember big pots of chicken and homemade noodles on cold nights that made my tummy feel warm and soothed. Sunday dinner always included chicken no matter what else was served. In my Grandmother's day, not to own chickens was to be deprived. As a child, there was something magical about gathering up freshly laid eggs and day dreaming about the wonders that Grandma would perform with them. Perhaps her wonderful rich, butter yellow pound cake on zabaglione, an italian pudding, so light it felt like a cloud in one's mouth. Or there might be a fresh vegetable frittata for lunch. To this day there is nothing that tastes quite as good as fresh laid eggs. When the good Lord created the chicken, he gave us all a princely gift.

Chicken a la P.W.

This dish was created for Paul Wafford (P.W.) one of the great winemakers of California and a fine cook in his own right. Paul is also a gifted port maker and the port I used in this recipe was a Reserved 1983 Vintage St Amant Port that Paul made. The flavor produced by blending the Cabernet, Port and the currant jelly is a perfect match for the cheesy nut flavor of the chicken stuffing.

1/4 lb. Roquefort cheese, crumbled into small pieces
1/2 cup finely chopped celery
1/4 cup finely chopped walnuts
4 half chicken breasts, boned, skinned and flattened
1/4 c. sifted all-purpose flour
2 Tbsps. corn oil
2 Tbsps. butter
2/3 cup Cabernet Sauvignon
2/3 cup port
2 Tbsps. red current jelly
1 cup cream

In a small bowl, combine Roquefort, celery and walnuts. Form into 4 rolls, about 3 inches long. Roll each piece of cheese in a chicken breast, turning ends in before last turn. Fasten with toothpick. Refrigerate at least 1 hour or until cheese mixture is firm. Heat oil and half of the butter in a large heavy skillet. Coat chicken rolls in flour and cook until golden and keep warm. Add Cabernet and port to skillet. Turn heat to high and bring wine to a boil. Lower heat and reduce liquid to half. Add jelly and cook until jelly is dissolved. Add cream and bring to a boil. Divide sauce between 4 warm plates. Add a chicken roll to each plate. Serve at once. Serves 4.

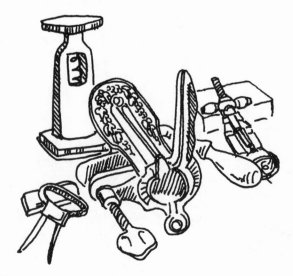

Apricot Glazed Chicken Breast

Fruit wines are becoming more widely available across the country. They have been produced in California for many years and Oregon, Washington, Ohio and Florida are just a few states making pure fruit wines.

4 whole chicken breasts, skinned, boned and cut in
*   halves*
2 Tbsps. olive oil
2 Tbsps. butter
1 medium white onion, coarsely chopped
1 large green bell pepper, stemmed, seeded and ribs
*   removed, cut into 1/4" strips*
2 large cloves garlic, minced
1 cup apricot wine
1/4 cup soy sauce
2 Tbsps. honey
1/4 cup brown sugar
1 bay leaf
Salt and pepper to taste
12 dried apricot halves

In a large heavy skillet, heat oil until haze forms. Add butter and melt. Add chicken breasts and brown on both sides. Transfer breasts to platter and set aside. Loosen and brown bits from bottom and sides of skillet and add onions, peppers and garlic. Saute just until onions are transparent. Add apricot wine, soy sauce, honey, brown sugar and bay leaf. Season with salt and pepper. Bring to a boil, lower heat and simmer 2 minutes. Return chicken breasts, cover and simmer for 30 minutes. Remove lid, add dried apricots and simmer another 15 minutes to reduce sauce. Remove bay leaf and discard. Serves 6. No substitute for apricot wine.

Tarragon Chicken

1–2 1/2 to 3 lb. chicken, cut up. Reserve neck and
*   giblets for stock or soup*
Salt and pepper to taste
1 Tbsp. olive oil
2 Tbsps. butter
3 fresh green onions, white part only, sliced
2 Tbsps fresh tarragon, finely minced
3/4 cup Gewurztraminer

Sprinkle chicken with salt and pepper. Heat olive oil until a haze forms in a large skillet. Add butter and melt. Add chicken and brown on both sides. Remove chicken and keep warm. Add onions and saute 2 to 3 minutes. Add tarragon and Gewurztraminer. Stir to dissolve any brown particles clinging to the skillet. Return chicken to skillet and cover. Cook 15 minutes, uncover and continue to cook, basting often, about 15 minutes. Remove to platter and spoon pan juices over chicken. Serves 4. Johannisberg Riesling may be substituted for the Gewurztraminer.

Country Chicken Stew

This delicious, hearty dish is quick to make and easy on the food budget, especially if you buy chickens when they are on sale.

3 Tbsps. olive oil
3 lbs. chicken, cut up
2–16 oz. cans whole tomatoes, broken up
2 cloves garlic, minced
1 tsp. salt
3/4 tsps. thyme leaves
3/4 tsps. fennel seed
1/2 tsp. coarse black pepper
1 bay leaf
2 cups celery, cut in 1" pieces
1 large potato, peeled and quartered lengthwise
1/2 cup dry vermouth

Heat oil in a large dutch oven, until a haze forms. add chicken and brown on all sides. Add tomatoes, garlic, salt, thyme, fennel, pepper and bay leaf. Bring to a boil. Reduce heat and simmer, covered, for 1/2 hour. Add celery, potato, and vermouth. Continue to simmer, uncovered, until chicken and vegetables are tender. About 15-20 minutes. Serves 6. I don't like to substitute for the vermouth in this dish, but if you must, use a good dry sherry.

Chicken Veronique

My friend Malcolm Hebert has been writing about food and wine for a lot of years with many cookbooks to his credit. One of my favorites is his CHAMPAGNE COOKBOOK. The following recipe is one I serve often and Malcolm has graciously allowed me to include it here.

2 Tbsps. salt
1/2 tsp. white pepper
3 Tbsps. flour
3 whole chicken breasts, skinned, boned and halved
5 Tbsps. butter
3/4 cup dry sparkling wine
3/4 cup seedless white grapes
3 Tbsps. blanched, sliced almonds

Mix salt, pepper and flour together and coat the breasts. Melt the butter in a large skillet and quickly but lightly brown the breasts on both sides. Add sparkling wine cover and cook 15 minutes. Add grapes and almonds and cook another 5 minutes. Serves 6. No substitute for the sparkling wine.

Rock Cornish Hens in Orange Sauce

4 rock cornish hens, cut in half
1 tsp. salt
All-purpose flour for dredging
1/4 tsp. cayenne pepper
2 Tbsps. olive oil
2 Tbsps. butter
1 cup Fume Blanc
1 Tbsp. arrowroot
1/2 cup Orange Marsala
1/2 cup orange juice
6 oz. (1/2 can) orange juice concentrate
2 tangerines, peeled and sectioned
1/2 cup almonds slivered and toasted

Season hens with salt and cayenne pepper. Dredge in flour. In a large heavy skillet heat oil until haze forms. Add butter and melt. Brown hens on both sides. Transfer to platter and set aside. Loosen brown bits from bottom and sides of skillet. Add Fume Blanc and bring to boil. Return hens to skillet, baste and cover skillet. Lower heat and simmer for 30 minutes. Again transfer hens to platter and set aside. Mix arrowroot with orange marsala and whisk into liquid in skillet. Add orange concentrate and cook until sauce thickens. Add tangerine sections and nuts and simmer another 5 minutes. Pour sauce over hens. Serves 6. Sauvignon Blanc may be substituted for the Fume Blanc. Any orange flavored liqueur may be substituted for the Orange Marsala.

Great Aunt Mary's Glazed Chicken

This is an example of an elegant dish that can be prepared in under 20 minutes. The flavors come together in a subtle yet zesty after taste.

Notes from Patti:

Hooray for progress!! Remember all those left over cans of tomato paste that got lost in the back of the refrigerator when you only needed a small amount to season? Now you can get tomato paste in a tube.

3 whole chicken breasts, skinned and halved
2 Tbsps. butter
Salt and pepper to taste
6 large cloves of garlic, finely minced
1/3 cup red wine vinegar
4 Tbsps. dry Marsala
1 Tbsp. tomato paste
2 Tbsps. Dijon style mustard
2/3 cup cream fraiche

Melt butter in a large heavy skillet over moderate heat. Add chicken and brown, 4 to 5 minutes on each side. Remove chicken and keep warm. Add garlic, vinegar and raise heat to high. Stir vigorously, scraping pan to loosen pieces in skillet. Reduce by 3/4. Combine dry marsala, tomato paste and mustard. Add to vinegar and cook 3 to 4 minutes, stirring constantly. Add the cream fraiche and stir until well blended. Pour glaze over chicken and serve immediately. No substitute for the Dry Marsala. Serves 4.

Great Aunt Mary's Cranberry
and Walnut Chicken

My Great Aunt Mary so loved the flavor of cranberries that we were always treated to many of her creations from her cranberry cake to this delicious chicken dish. She always said God meant cranberries to be used in lots of ways–not just a sauce!

1 broiler chicken, cut into pieces
1 tsp. salt
1/4 cup olive oil
2 Tbsps. butter
1 medium white onion, diced
1/4 tsp cinnamon
1/4 tsp. ginger
1 Tbsp. grated orange rind
1/2 cup orange juice
1/2 cup tawny port
2 cups fresh cranberries
3/4 cup chopped walnuts

Sprinkle chicken with salt. Heat oil and butter in a large skillet and brown chicken on both sides. Add onions, spices, orange rind, orange juice and port. Cover and simmer for 20 minutes. Add cranberries and walnuts and simmer uncovered for an additional 10 to 15 minutes. Serves 4. I especially like the flavor the tawny port lends to this dish, but any port such as Tinta Maderia is acceptable.

Turkey and Pasta
with Dry White Riesling

I love dishes like this one. It takes only 20 minutes from start to finish but tastes like you spent hours in the kitchen!

4 Tbsps. olive oil
2 large cloves garlic, finely minced
1 bunch (6) fresh green onions, chopped
1 bunch broccoli, cut into flowerettes
2 medium zucchini, sliced
1/4 lb. snow peas
1 carrot, julienned
1/2 cup a dry style White Riesling
2 cups cubed cooked turkey
2 Tbsps. fresh parsley, chopped
2 Tbsps. fresh basil, chopped
10 oz. hot, cooked fusilli (corkscrew pasta)
1 cup cream
Salt and pepper to taste
1/4 cup freshly grated parmesan cheese

Heat oil in a large dutch oven until a haze forms. Add garlic, onions, broccoli, zucchini, snow peas and carrots and saute 3 to 4 minutes. Add Riesling, turkey, parsley, and basil. Cover and simmer and additional 3 minutes. Add hot, cooked pasta and toss. Add cream and season with salt and pepper to taste. Add cheese and give a final toss. Serve with sourdough bread and the rest of the Riesling.

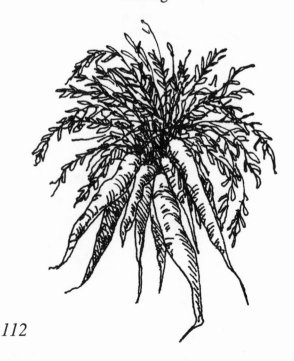

Lemon Chicken
with Gewurztraminer Sauce

6 chicken breast halves, boned and skinned
1/2 cup fresh squeezed lemon juice
1 large egg
2/3 cup all purpose flour
2/3 cup sourdough bread crumbs
3 tsps. grated lemon rind
2 tsps. chopped fresh dill or 1/2 tsp. dried dillweed
1 tsp. salt
4 Tbsps. olive oil
2 Tbsps. butter

Pour lemon juice into a glass baking dish. Add chicken breasts, cover and refrigerate 45 minutes. Turn chicken and refrigerate an additional 45 minutes. Remove chicken from marinade and pat dry with paper towels. Reserve marinade. Beat egg and 1/4 cup lemon marinade in shallow bowl. Set aside. Combine flour, bread crumbs, lemon rind, dill, salt and pepper in a plastic bag. Heat half of the oil and butter in a large heavy skillet. Dip each chicken breast in egg mixture, then shake in crumb mixture . Place in hot oil mixture. Cook until golden brown on one side (6 to 8 minutes). Add remaining oil and butter, turn chicken and cook an additional 8 minutes.

Gewurztraminer Sauce

2 cups chicken stock
2 cups Gewurztraminer
1/2 pint cream
3 Tbsps. COLD butter

Blot up all oil in the skillet with paper towels leaving any browned bits. Add chicken stock and reduce to one cup. Add Gewurztraminer and continue to reduce to 2 cups total liquid. Add cream and bring to a boil. Reduce heat to low and whisk in butter a little at a time. Each addition should be well incorporated before more butter is added. Spoon over chicken and serve at once.

Scallops of Chicken
with Sauvignon Blanc Sauce

This is one of may all time favorite chicken dishes because it is so fast to make (under 10 minutes). I often make it for luncheon guests at the winery. Whether you serve it for lunch or dinner, your family will love it for its taste and you will love how easy it is to make.

4 half chicken breasts, boned and skinned
1 tsp. salt
1/2 tsp. freshly ground black pepper
4 Tbsps. unsifted all-purpose flour
4 Tbsps. butter
2 shallots, finely chopped
1/2 cup Sauvignon Blanc
2 Tbsps. lemon juice
1 1/2 cups cream
4 thin slices of lemon

Sprinkle chicken breasts with salt and pepper. Place flour in a paper bag. Add chicken breasts, one at a time and shake to coat completely. Place chicken breasts between 2 sheets of waxed paper and pound to flatten. Heat oven to 325°F. Heat butter in a large, heavy skillet. Add chicken breasts and cook until golden on both sides. Transfer chicken to baking dish and place in oven for 5 minutes. Add shallots to skillet and saute until tender. Add wine, lemon juice and cream. Bring to a boil. Lower heat and simmer for 1 minute. Divide sauce between 4 warm plates. Add a chicken breast to each plate and garnish with lemon slice. Serve at once. Serves 4.

Patti's Chicken Chardonnay

This wonderful dish is the result of a fine bottle of Chardonnay given to me by Bill Ryan when I visited the beautiful Rhine House at Beringer Winery in St. Helena, California last year. It was a delightfully rainy spring day and Bill graciously took time to show me parts of the Rhine House I had not seen before. Bill also took me to visit their kitchen and taste a chocolate treat created by a charming young lady –it was decadent! I had a great time–Thanks Bill!

2 whole chicken breasts, boned, skinned, halved and
   flattened
2 Tbsps. butter
1 1/2 cups double strength chicken stock
1 cup Chardonnay
1/2 pint cream
3 Tbsps. COLD butter, cut into 6 pieces
Dash of white pepper

Brown chicken breasts in butter on each side in a large heavy skillet. Remove to platter and keep warm. Add chicken stock to skillet and reduce to 2/3 cup. Add Chardonnay and continue reducing to 3/4 cup total liquid. Add cream and whisk in butter, one piece at a time. Pour over chicken breasts and serve immediately. Serves 4.

115

Grandma's Roast Chicken with Pesto

This is a dish that has been in our family for as long as I can remember. Preparation is simple–the result is elegant.

4 cups fresh basil, tightly packed
4 large cloves garlic
1/4 cup olive oil
2 Tbsps. butter
1/2 cup pine nuts
1 roasting chicken, 5 to 6 pounds
3 medium white onions, peeled
1/2 tsp. salt
3 Tbsps. butter
1/2 cup dry sherry

Place basil and garlic in a food processor fitted with a steel blade. Turn on processor and add olive oil through feed tube. Process until basil and garlic are pureed. Add butter and pine nuts and process 10 seconds. Set aside. Rinse chicken with cold water and pat dry. Sprinkle cavity of chicken with salt. Gently loosen the skin of the chicken by inserting your fingers between the skin and body of the bird. Continue to loosen as much skin as possible around the back and breast. Spread the pesto mixture between the skin and body of the chicken until you have used all the pesto. Place onions in the cavity. Pull skin over cavity and secure with a metal skewer or toothpicks. Turn wings under and tie legs together. Place chicken on a roasting rack in roasting pan. Melt butter in a small saucepan. Add sherry and blend together. Baste chicken thoroughly and place in preheated 325°F oven. Roast 20 minutes per pound. Baste frequently with butter and sherry mixture. When chicken is fully cooked, remove from oven and let sit 15 to 20 minutes before carving. Serves 6. No substitute for good sherry in this recipe.

Petto Di Pollo a la Florentina

This dish will turn any party into a memorable evening and family and guests will ask for it often. The recipe can be cut in half.

Notes from Patti:

This dish sounds complicated and time consuming but with a little planning it's easy. The stuffing can be prepared up to 2 days ahead and refrigerated. Be sure to bring the rolls to room temperature before cooking. My favorite garnish is a few fresh basil leaves topped with a tomato rose. To make the rose, peel a large firm tomato, starting at the top and carefully peel in a single spiral to the bottom of the tomato. The spiral will fall into the shape of a rose.

1 cup fresh bread crumbs
2 oz. prosciutto, chopped
1/2 cup prepared pesto
1/4 cup pine nuts
4 large cloves garlic, finely minced
2 oz. sun-dried tomatoes, coarsely chopped
1/4 cup chicken stock
2 egg yolks, slightly beaten
2 Tbsps. heavy cream
8 whole chicken breasts, skinned, split, boned and
* pounded*
4 Tbsps. olive oil
4 Tbsps. butter
1 1/2 cups Chardonnay
2 cups chicken stock
1 1/2 cups heavy cream
1/4 tsp. freshly ground black pepper

In a mixing bowl, combine bread crumbs, prosciutto, pesto, pine nuts, garlic and tomatoes. In a small bowl, combine chicken stock, egg yolk and cream and whisk until blended. Pour over stuffing mixture and toss. Refrigerate 1 hour. Spread 1 tablespoon stuffing down the center of each breast half. Roll up and secure with wooden toothpicks. In a large heavy skillet, heat 2 tablespoons oil until haze forms. Add butter. Place 8 rolls in the skillet and saute until lightly browned. About 4 minutes on each side. Transfer to an ovenproof platter and keep warm in a preheated 200°F oven. Repeat with remaining oil, butter and chicken rolls. Scrape bottom and side of skillet to loosen any browned bits. Add Chardonnay and boil for 5 minutes. Add broth and continue to boil until liquid is reduced by half. Strain and return to skillet. Add cream and pepper, reduce heat and simmer 10 minutes. Spoon sauce over chicken rolls. Serves 16. You may substitute Sauvignon Blanc for the Chardonnay but the Chardonnay gives a more intense flavor to the sauce.

Pollo Con Frutta Secca

Dried fruits have always been an integral part of the cooking of Northern Italy for both the flavor and the color they give to poultry. This is a classic dish often served on feast days.

3 to 3 1/2 lb. chicken, cut into pieces
4 large cloves of garlic, finely minced
2 tsps. dried oregano
1/4 cup olive oil
1/4 cup red wine vinegar
1 cup pitted prunes
1/2 cup dried apricots
2 bay leaves
1/2 cup pitted green olives, sliced
2 Tbsps. capers
1 Tbsps. caper juice
1/2 cup brown sugar
3/4 cup Chardonnay

In a large bowl, combine chicken, garlic, oregano, olive oil, vinegar, prunes, apricots, bay leaves, olives, capers and caper juice. Cover and refrigerate 24 hours. Preheat oven to 350°F. Arrange chicken in a single layer in a shallow baking pan and spoon marinade evenly over chicken. Sprinkle with brown sugar and pour Chardonnay around chicken. Bake 45 minutes, basting every 15 minutes. With a slotted spoon, remove chicken, fruit, olives and capers to a serving platter. Pour several spoonfuls of pan juices over chicken. Serve remaining pan juices in a sauce boat. Serves 4. White Burgundy may be substituted for Chardonnay.

Pollo Di Piedmonte

The Cabernet Sauvignon adds a rich, almost mahogany color to the sauce and an elegant after taste of black currents. This dish is easy to prepare and fit for guests with discriminating taste!

1 fryer, 2 1/2 to 3 lbs., cut into pieces
4 Tbsps. olive oil
4 Tbsps. butter
1/2 cup Cabernet Sauvignon
1 lb. fresh tomatoes, peeled, seeded and coarsely
  chopped
1/4 tsp. white pepper
8 to 10 fresh basil leaves, minced

Rinse chicken pieces and pat dry. Heat oil and butter in a large, heavy skillet. Brown chicken pieces on all sides and cook until tender. Remove chicken to platter and keep warm. Loosen any bits adhering to the pan. Add wine and boil until wine is reduced to half. Add tomatoes, pepper, and fresh basil. Cook for 5 minutes over moderate heat. Return chicken to skillet and spoon sauce over pieces. Cook additional 5 minutes. Serves 4. No substitute for Cabernet Sauvignon.

Chicken Tonnato

In Italy there is a classic dish called VITELLO TONNATO, which means veal with tuna sauce. I have heard many stories about this dish and somehow the impression has always been left with me that to serve this dish was showing off ones' wealth since veal has always been expensive. Grandma always said it was possible to capture the visual appeal, flavor and texture with chicken. This is her version of VITELLO TONNATO, and it's been a classic in our family for many years.

4 large whole chicken breasts, bones, skinned and
   halved
1/4 cup olive oil
1 large onion, sliced
1–3 oz. can anchovy fillets, drained
1–7 oz. can white tuna, drained and broken
   into chunks
3/4 cup Chardonnay
2 cups chicken broth
3 large cloves garlic, crushed
4 stalks celery, with leaves, sliced
1 large carrot
6 sprigs parsley
Salt to taste
1/2 tsp. whole black peppercorns
2 cups mayonnaise, preferably homemade
3 Tbsps. lemon juice
4 cups cold cooked rice
Capers
Radish roses

Notes from Patti:

This dish may sound more difficult than it really is. It is strictly a do ahead dish, therefore wonderful for dinner parties!

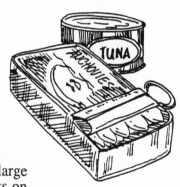

Pat chicken breasts dry with paper towels. Heat oil in a large dutch oven until hot but not smoking. Brown chicken breasts on both sides. Add onions, anchovies, tuna, Chardonnay, broth, garlic, celery, carrots, parsley, salt and peppercorns. Bring to a boil, cover, reduce heat and simmer 20 to 25 minutes, until fork tender. Gently remove chicken breasts to a shallow, glass baking dish. Cover with the hot stock. Cool to room temperature and refrigerate over night. Next day lift chicken from stock and refrigerate alone. Strain stock and discard vegetables. In a food processor, fitted with a plastic mixing blade, or in a blender, place mayonnaise, 1 cup stock and lemon juice. Process just until smooth. The sauce should be a little thicker than heavy cream. Adjust seasoning if necessary. Spread a thick layer of cold cooked rice over a serving platter. Arrange chicken on rice, cover with sauce and sprinkle with capers. Arrange 5 or 6 radish roses around platter. Serves 6. Sauvignon Blanc may be substituted for the Chardonnay.

Chicken San Joaquin

Frank and Grace Ann Verducco are among my favorite people in the whole wide world. Between "his and hers" they have raised nine wonderful children. Frank and Grace Anne are both experts in bonsai gardening and their Hour of Sunshine Nursery is a wonderful place to while away an hour or two. For you and I this recipe means leftovers–for the Verducco family this is just an average meal.

Notes from Patti:

If you're not having a party you may cut the recipe in half, but leftovers are great.

2–2 1/2 lbs. chicken cut up
Salt and freshly ground pepper to taste
2/3 cup olive oil
1 1/2 cups Gewurztraminer
3/4 lbs. fresh mushrooms, thickly sliced
3 shallots
1 1/2 cups pitted black olives
1–#10 can Italian plum tomatoes, broken into pieces

Season chicken with salt and pepper. Heat oil in a large heavy skillet until haze forms and brown chicken. Transfer chicken to a large ovenproof casserole. Pour of oil and reserve. Scrape bottom and sides to loosen any brown bits and add Gewurztraminer. Bring to a boil and continue to scrap skillet. Simmer 2 to 3 minutes. Pour Gewurztraminer over chicken. Return oil to skillet and saute mushrooms and shallots just until mushrooms are brown. Drain excess oil and add mushrooms and shallots to chicken. Add olives and tomatoes. Cover and place in a preheated 375°F oven. Bake 45 minutes. Serve over hot rice. Serves 8-10 hungry people. You may substitute Johannisberg Riesling for the Gewurztraminer.

Meat

Animal meat, in one form or another has been man's most dependable food source since the dawning of time. His first efforts at tool making had to do with implements to help him slaughter his prey and cut it into more manageable portions. He also learned that every part of the animal was necessary to his survival.

Today, although we are not so dependent on meat, we still have a great love for it. According to the Department of Commerce, each of us consume an average of 170 pounds of meat every year.

As a child, we always had a wide variety of meat. Pappa raised chickens and rabbits and a neighbor would buy pigs and lambs and share them. We did have beef but I don't remember it as the predominant meat in our diet.

Wine is a natural ingredient to pair with all meats. Not only does wine enhance the flavor of meat, the natural acids help to soften and tenderize. Some cheaper cuts, especially beef, have wonderful flavor but are less desirable because of the toughness of the meat. With these cuts, wine is not just desirable, it is essential.

Veal with Seafood Sauce

While this isn't an inexpensive dish, it is foolproof and quick to prepare. When you want to pamper yourself and someone you love, try this one!

Notes from Patti:

Keep in mind that Madeira is not just one wine, but a whole company of wines, varying from very dry to very sweet. For cooking Madeira has a remarkable flavor that even the finest sherry or Marsala cannot replace. Like sherry and Marsala, Madeira is fortified and will last for a very long time.

4–3 oz. slices boneless veal
Salt and white pepper to taste
All-purpose flour, for dredging
2 Tbsps. oil
3/4 lb fresh mushrooms, sliced
2 cups heavy cream
1/4 cup dry Madeira
1/2 stick butter, cut into 12 pieces
1/2 cup cooked crabmeat
8 large shrimp, peeled and deveined

Pound veal to a thickness of 1/4". Season with salt and pepper and dredge lightly in flour. Shake off excess flour. Heat oil in a large skillet until haze forms. Add veal and brown quickly, no more than 45-50 seconds, on each side. Transfer veal to platter and keep warm. Add mushrooms to skillet and saute about 5 minutes. Add cream and Madeira and reduce until thickened, about 15 minutes. Season with salt and pepper. Stir in butter, one piece at at time, whisking briskly and incorporating each piece completely before adding more. Add crabmeat and shrimp and heat through, about 1 minute. Pour over veal and serve at once. Serves 4. There is no substitute for dry Madeira.

Veal Beverly

Beverly Bargetto is one of the strongest women I've ever known. After the sudden death of her husband, Lawrence, she chose to continue the Bargetto Family Winery with the participation of her children. She is a busy lady and doesn't have a lot of time for the kitchen. This is a favorite because it is easy to prepare and elegant to serve.

*1 bunch fresh green onions, with 1/4 of the
   green stems, chopped*
2 Tbsps. butter
1/4 lb. prosciutto (Italian ham) cut into julienne strips
2 Tbsps. port
Rind of 1/2 lemon, grated
1/2 cup Fume Blanc
1 cup veal or beef stock
1 tsp. salt
1/2 tsp. pepper
1/2 cup flour
1 1/2 lbs. veal, cut into scallopini and pounded thin
2 Tbsps. olive oil
1 Tbsp. butter
2 Tbsps. COLD BUTTER, cut into 8 pieces

Notes from Patti:

The sauce, up to the point of adding the cold butter, may be made early in the day and finished just before use. You may substitute chicken stock for the veal or beef stock and serve over sauted chicken breast.

Saute onions in butter in a medium saucepan for about 1 minute. Add prosciutto, port and lemon rind. Cook over medium flame for an additional minute. In a separate saucepan reduce Fume Blanc and stock by half and add to onion/ham mixture. Cover and set aside. Mix salt and pepper into flour. Dredge veal in flour. Heat oil and butter in a large heavy skillet until very hot, being careful not to burn the butter. Add veal and cook about 2 minutes on each side. Blot up any excessive oil left in skillet. Set aside. Bring onion/ham mixture to a boil. Whisk in cold butter 1 piece at a time. Pour sauce over veal and cook just until veal is hot. Serves 4. Sauvignon Blanc may be substituted for Fume Blanc.

Veal Marsala

This dish is fit for royalty. I've never served this to anyone who didn't love it, and again, it's so easy to prepare.

Notes from Patti:

This is one of my very favorite dishes, but I like it more lemony. I often increase the lemon juice to 4 teaspoons and garnish with twists of lemon slices. To save even more time, pound the veal in the morning and refrigerate until ready to cook.

8 veal scallops
1/2 tsp. salt
1/2 tsp. coarsely ground black pepper
All-purpose flour, for dredging
4 Tbsps. butter
2 fresh green onions, white parts only, sliced
1 large clove garlic, minced
1 Tbsp. capers
1/2 cup Dry Marsala wine
1/2 cup chicken stock
2 tsps. lemon juice

Place scallops between wax paper and using a wooden mallet, pound to 1/4" thickness. Season with salt and pepper and coat with flour, shaking off any excess. Melt 2 tablespoons butter in a heavy skillet. Add 4 scallops and cook 30 seconds on each side. Transfer to a platter and keep warm. Add remaining butter to skillet and cook remaining scallops in the same way. Transfer to platter. Loosen any brown bits from bottom and sides of skillet, add onions and garlic and saute about 1 minute. Add capers, Marsala and chicken stock. Bring to a boil and reduce to half. Stir in lemon juice and pour over veal. Serves 4. No substitute for Dry Marsala.

Lemoned Veal

1 lb. veal scallops, pounded thin
All-purpose flour, for dredging
2 Tbsps. olive oil
2 Tbsps. butter
4 fresh green onions, white part only, thinly sliced
1/2 cup Chardonnay
2 Tbsps. fresh lemon juice (I like more)
1 tsp. chopped fresh parsley
6 thin slices lemon

Dredge scallops in flour. Shake off excess. In a large heavy skillet, heat 1 tablespoon of oil and 1 tablespoon butter until haze forms. Add scallops to skillet without crowding and sprinkle with half the green onions. Cook 10 to 15 seconds. Turn and cook another 10 to 15 seconds. Transfer to heated platter and keep warm. Add remaining oil and butter and repeat with remaining scallops and onions. Return cooked scallops to skillet, add Chardonnay and lemon juice to skillet. Cook 1 minute. Transfer to platter and keep warm. Add parsley to skillet. Cook, stirring constantly, 2 minutes or until slightly thicker. Pour sauce over scallops and garnish with lemon. Serves 6. Sauvignon Blanc may be substituted for Chardonnay.

Grandma's Zinfandel Beef

This is a dish our family has always loved. The salt pork lends a savory flavor that sets it apart from all the others.

4 oz. piece salt pork, rind removed and cubed
1 Tbsp. olive oil
2 lbs. beef stew meat, cubed
2 carrots, sliced
1 large onion, diced
Salt and pepper to taste
2 Tbsp. all-purpose flour
1 1/2 cups beef stock
1 1/2 cups Zinfandel
1/4 cup tomato sauce
2 large cloves garlic, minced
1 tsp. dry thyme
1 bay leaf, crumbled
1 lb. fresh mushrooms, halved

Notes from Patti:

At one dinner, a guest, thinking she was complimenting my grandmother, compared this dish to a classic French beef. My grandmother promptly replied that it was common knowledge that the French had learned everything they knew from the Northern Italians!

Drop salt pork into 1 quart boiling water and boil for 10 to15 minutes. Remove with slotted spoon and dry on paper towels. Using a heavy dutch oven, saute salt pork in olive oil to render the fat. Remove salt pork and reserve. Saute beef cubes, a few at a time, in the hot oil, until browned. Add to salt pork. Heat oven to 450°F. Saute carrots and onions in the dutch oven. Add the vegetables to the meat and discard the leftover fat. Do not scrape bottom of dutch oven. Return salt pork, beef and vegetables to dutch oven. Sprinkle with salt, pepper and flour. Toss lightly to coat the beef with flour. Place dutch oven, uncovered, in oven for 5 minutes to brown the flour. Toss again and continue to brown another 5 minutes. Reduce oven temperature to 325°F and remove dutch oven to top of stove. Add beef stock, Zinfandel, tomato sauce, garlic, thyme and bay leaf. Cover, heat to simmer and return to oven for 3 to 3 1/2 hours, until meat is fork tender. When beef is done, add mushrooms, cover and let sit for 5 minutes. Sauce should be just thick enough to coat a spoon. If too thick, thin with about 1/4 cup Zinfandel. If too thin, dissolve 1 teaspoon arrowroot in a tablespoon of zinfandel and stir into mixture. Serve over lightly buttered, homemade noodles. Serves 6. No substitute for Zinfandel.

Perfect Prime Ribs of Beef
with Mushroom Sauce

Notes from Patti:

Arrowroot is a wonderful thickening agent. It will never lump in either hot or cold sauces and it does not leave an after taste as flour or cornstarch will. I buy it in bulk from a health food store. Much less expensive than prepackaged arrowroot in grocery stores.

It seems in the last three years, every food editor in the country has come up with a revolutionary "new" way to prepare prime ribs of beef. In fact, there is nothing new about this method. It was the only way my grandmother cooked her prime rib.

Choose a rib prime beef, about 6 pounds. Leaving bones intact, have your butcher roll and tie it. When ready to cook, bring the roast to room temperature. Rub the roast generously with salt and pepper. Preheat the oven to 375°F for 15 minutes. Place the roast, fat side up, in a shallow pan. Put the roast in the oven and cook for EXACTLY 1 hour. Turn off the heat and leave roast in the oven for 4 hours. DO NOT, UNDER ANY CIRCUMSTANCE, OPEN THE OVEN DOOR. 1 hour before serving, turn the oven to 300°F and continue to cook for 45 minutes. Remove to carving board and let rest for 15 to 20 minutes before carving. It is IMPORTANT to follow these directions to the letter if you want a perfect medium rare prime rib. Serves 6.

Mushroom Sauce

> 2 cups Cabernet Sauvignon
> 1 cup Dry Marsala
> 2 Tbsps. lemon juice
> 1 lb. fresh mushrooms, sliced in fourths
> 1 tsp. arrowroot

Pour off fat from prime rib pan. Add Cabernet Sauvignon and deglaze, scraping any browned bits from bottom and sides of pan. Bring to a boil and simmer until wine is reduced to half. Add Marsala and lemon juice and continue to simmer for 5 minutes. Add mushrooms and cook 3-5 minutes or until mushrooms are fork tender. Add arrowroot and stir just until sauce is slightly thickened.

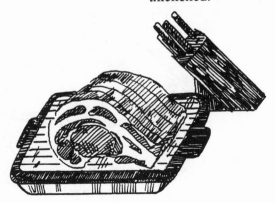

Patti's Filet Mignons

We were just about ready to complete this book when I remembered Patti's wonderful filet recipe. Should we save it for a future book? No, we couldn't wait to share it with you!–*Jill*

4–4 oz. filet mignons
2 Tbsps. peppercorns, crushed
2 Tbsps. olive oil
1 Tbsp. butter
2 cloves garlic, slightly crushed
1 cup beef stock
1 cup Cabernet Sauvignon
1/2 cup heavy cream
2 Tbsps. Dijon style mustard
2 Tbsps. VERY COLD butter, cut into 4 pieces
10 large mushrooms, thickly sliced

Press crushed peppercorns into both sides of steaks and refrigerate for one hour. Heat oil in a large heavy skillet until a haze forms. Stir in butter, add garlic and stir until browned. Remove and discard garlic. Add filets, being careful not to crowd. Cook until crisp on outside, about 1 minute on each side, but still pink inside. Remove to platter and keep warm. Add beef stock to pan drippings and reduce to half. Add Cabernet Sauvignon and continue to reduce until about 1 cup liquid remains. Blend in cream and mustard. Whisk in one piece of butter at a time, being careful each piece of butter is completely incorporated before adding additional butter. Add mushrooms and cook an additional minute. Pour over steaks and serve at once. Serves 4.

Notes from Patti:

For those of you who know me, you have heard me espouse the use of fine wine in food a number of times. This recipe is a perfect example of this philosophy. Aside from the fact that a good Cabernet not only stands up to but enhances the peppery flavor of these steaks for which you have paid top dollar, why then, would you take a chance on any but the very best ingredients to complete the dish? Yes, I have asked you to use one full cup of this expensive wine (for this expensive meat), but quality always speaks for itself. When you taste this sauce, you will understand why I demand the very best quality in both the food and the wine.

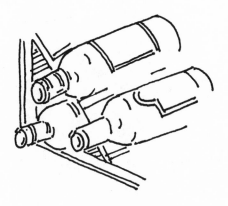

Beef Stroganoff

This is an elegant little dish that can be made in no time at all with ingredients you probably have on hand or can easily purchase.

1 1/2 lbs. boneless sirloin
1/4 cup all-purpose flour
2 Tbsps. olive oil
2 Tbsps. butter
1 clove garlic, minced
6 fresh green onions, sliced with half the greens
1/2 lb. mushrooms, quartered
1/2 cup Petite Sirah
2 cups sour cream
2 tsps.Dijon style mustard
2 tsps.Worcestershire sauce
1/2 tsp. salt
1/2 tsp. cracked pepper
1 Tbsp. dried dill weed

Notes from Patti:

Sauces made with sour cream can be reheated if done with care. Transfer dish to a casserole, with cover, and place in a pan filled with 1" boiling water. Heat in a 350°F oven for 45 minutes.

Partially freeze meat to make it easier to cut across the grain into 1/4" wide strips. Cut down the center of each strip into approximately 1/2" wide pieces. Toss meat with flour. In a large skillet, heat half of oil and butter until haze forms. Brown about 1/3 of meat strips until brown on both sides, over high heat. Remove meat and add remaining oil and butter and continue to brown meat in batches. Remove meat and add garlic, onion and mushrooms. Saute until onion is transparent. Remove from pan. Add Petite Sirah to skillet and heat, stirring to dislodge and scrape up all brown bits from pan. Bring to a boil over high heat and boil 3 minutes or until alcohol has burned off. Reduce heat and add remaining ingredients, stirring until sauce is well blended. Add meat, garlic, onions and mushrooms and mix thoroughly. Heat until sauce is piping hot. Serve over hot, buttered noodles. Serves 4. Barbera may be substituted for Petite Sirah.

Beef Paprika

This is a lovely old dish whose flavor is greatly enhanced by the spicy flavor of Madeira.

1 1/2 lbs top round steak, sliced into thin
bite-size pieces
1/2 tsp. salt
1/4 tsp. pepper
6 Tbsps. butter
1/2 lb. mushrooms, thickly sliced
2 large onions, thinly sliced
2 large cloves garlic, minced
1/4 cup tomato paste
1/4 cup Dijon style mustard
3 cups beef stock
1/3 cup dry Madeira
1 heaping tablespoon sweet paprika
1 cup dairy sour cream
1 lb. wide egg noodles, preferably homemade

Notes from Patti:

Madeira wine varies greatly from quite dry to sweet as do Marsalas. For most recipes, other than desserts, the drier styles are more desirable.

Pat meat dry with paper toweling. Sprinkle with salt and pepper. Melt 2 tablespoons of the butter in a large dutch oven. Quickly brown meat on each side in a single layer. Transfer to platter. Brown remaining meat, adding more butter as necessary. Add remaining butter to pot and saute mushrooms, onions, and garlic until mushrooms are tender-crisp. Transfer to a separate plate. Add tomato paste and mustard and mix thoroughly. Slowly add 2 cups of the beef broth, stirring constantly to make a smooth sauce. Stir in Madeira and paprika. Return mushrooms, onions, and garlic to pot. Simmer uncovered for 10 minutes. Place sour cream in a bowl and slowly whisk in remaining cup of beef broth until mixture is smooth. Pour into pot, stirring constantly for 4 to 5 minutes. Add meat and cooked noodles and heat to serving temperature. Serves 6 generously. Dry Marsala may be substituted for Madeira, but this dish really deserves the Madeira.

Stuffed London Broil

Papa rarely cooked, but once or twice a year he would prepare his favorite London Broil. The vinegar marinade gives the meat a zesty flavor unlike anything I've tasted.

3 lbs. London Broil
8 slices bacon, cut in fourths
1 large onion, coarsely chopped
1 bell pepper, seeded and coarsely diced
1/2 cup finely chopped parsley
1 Tbsp. peppercorns
Salt and pepper to taste

1/4 cup red wine vinegar
2 large cloves garlic, minced as fine as possible
2 Tbsps. olive oil
1/2 tsp. thyme
1 tsp. tarragon

Cut into steak from one side making a deep horizontal slit like a pocket. Cook bacon, in a large skillet, until crisp. Drain off fat. Stir in onions and pepper and cook until tender-crisp. Add parsley and peppercorns. Sprinkle meat inside and out with salt and pepper and stuff with bacon mixture. Secure opening with metal skewers or large sandwich type toothpicks. Mix vinegar, oil, thyme and tarragon. Place meat in shallow glass baking dish and brush all sides with marinade. Marinate for 1 to 2 hours. Cook meat on barbecue grill 4 inches from medium hot coals 15 minutes on each side. Brush often with marinade. You may also broil the meat in your oven following the above instructions. Serves 6 generously.

Fruited Loin of Pork

White Zinfandels are relatively new in the wine market having been produced for 6-8 years. It has become so popular that most California wineries make it. White Zinfandels are beautiful to the eye, the cold or ranges from pale salmon to deep pinks, and is so easy to drink. If well made it pleases almost everyone. Residual sugars vary greatly from 1-2%. I prefer about 1% which gives you a lovely fruity taste without a sweet coating in the mouth.

4 lb. boneless loin roast, prepared for stuffing (ask your
butcher to cut a deep pocket lengthwise in the roast)
1 cup pitted prunes, coarsely chopped
1 cup dried apricots, coarsely chopped
1/2 cup walnuts, coarsely chopped
3 large cloves garlic, sliced
Salt and coarsely ground pepper to taste
1/4 lb. butter, softened
1 Tbsp. dried thyme
1 1/2 to 2 cups White Zinfandel
2 Tbsps. white corn syrup

Mix prunes, apricots and walnuts. Stuff the pocket with fruit mixture. Make deep slits in the roast and insert the garlic. Tie the roast securely with twine and rub with salt and pepper. Place the roast in a shallow baking pan and brush generously with butter. Sprinkle with thyme. Stir corn syrup into White Zinfandel and pour over meat. Preheat oven to 350°F and place pan on middle rack and bake for 1 1/2 hours (about 20 minutes per pound) basting often. When roast is done, remove from oven and loosely cover with foil. Let stand 20 minutes. Cut into thin slices and arrange on platter and spoon pan juices over slices. Garnish with parsley and any other fresh herbs that you may have. Serves 6. No substitute for White Zinfandel.

Sherried Lamb Chops

When you're tired but hungry for a good meal, this is the perfect dish. It only takes minutes to prepare and tastes sensational.

8 loin lamb chops, trimmed of all fat
2 Tbsps. flour
2 Tbsps. olive oil
2 Tbsps. butter
1 red bell pepper, cored, seeded and cut into thin strips
1 green bell pepper, cored, seeded and cut
  into thin strips
1 medium onion, sliced thin
3 cloves garlic, minced
1/2 cup dry sherry
2 medium tomatoes, seeded and diced
1 Tbsp. red wine vinegar
2 Tbsp. minced parsley
1 lemon, cut into wedges

Dust chops with flour and season with pepper. Heat olive oil and butter in a heavy skillet over high heat. Brown chops on both sides until lightly brown. Remove chops from heat and keep warm. Lower heat and add peppers, onion and garlic and saute until tender. Stir in sherry, tomatoes and vinegar. Bring to simmer. Return chops to skillet and baste frequently with sauce until chops are done, about 5 minutes. Sprinkle with parsley and garnish with lemon wedges. Serves 4. No substitute for dry sherry.

Pomegranate Leg of Lamb

1–5 to 6 lb. leg of lamb
12 large cloves of garlic, cut in half lengthwise
1 tsp. salt
1/2 tsp. coarsely ground black pepper
2 large onions, coarsely chopped
15 fresh basil leaves, (must be fresh), torn into small
   pieces
1–750 ml. bottle of pomegranate wine
1/3 cup olive oil

Make 24 slits all over the leg of lamb. Insert 1/2 cloves of garlic in each slit. Rub leg with salt and pepper and place in a large heavy duty plastic bag. Put onions, basil, pomegranate wine and oil in a large bowl and whisk until well blended. Pour over lamb and close bag with a tie twist. Shake and refrigerate for 24 hours. Turn once or twice each day. Remove lamb from marinade and place in a shallow roasting pan. Preheat oven to 325°F. Roast lamb 20 minutes per pound. Strain marinade and discard onions and basil. Brush lab every 20 minutes with marinade. Twenty minutes before lamb is done, pour remaining marinade into a saucepan and bring to a boil. Reduce to half. Serve with lamb. Serves 8. No substitute for pomegranate wine.

Jerry Predika's Potato Sausage

Master sausage-making chef Jerry Predika has collected hundreds of ethnic recipes from countries around the globe and passes them onto you in his last work THE SAUSAGE MAKING COOKBOOK. Jerry teaches wine appreciation and sausage making. I count him among my friends.

Notes from Patti:

This sausage freezes well up to 4 months. But I prefer to make smaller batches as needed. You can increase or decrease this recipe easily. Casings may be purchased from your neighborhood butcher shop. If their not available most butchers would be happy to order them for you. This sausage can also be made into patties.

10 lbs. medium ground pork butt
6 large onions, coarsely chopped
3 Tbsps. salt
3 tsps. white pepper
1 tsp. ground allspice
1 tsp. ground mace
1 tsp. ground nutmeg
9 large cloves garlic, finely minced
2 Tbsps. sugar
2 cups Gewurztraminer
5 lbs potatoes, grated
2 Tbsps. lemon juice

Mix all ingredients together thoroughly except the potatoes and lemon juice. Sprinkle the lemon juice over potatoes and let stand 5 minutes. Mix potatoes with meat mixture and stuff into hog casings. Bake in a 350°F oven for 1 hour. Makes 15 pounds of sausage. A medium dry White Riesling may be substituted for the Gewurztraminer.

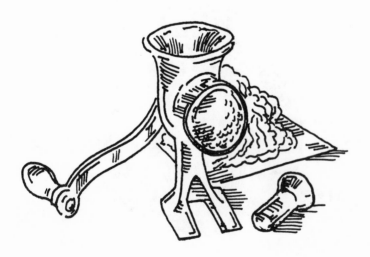

Desserts

Desserts are not primary to our diets but something we do to please ourselves. Some people feel deprived, or depending on your point of view, depraved, if they don't have some form of dessert every single night. I actually know people who put their bodies through hours of excruciating exercise to justify a triple icecream sundae with fudge sauce and whipped cream.

In our family we most often had fruit for dessert during the week, but on the weekend, there was always some wonderful surprise from grandma. She called them her "little rewards". As a child I never questioned her, but as I grew older, I began to understand. Grandma felt we worked hard during the week and for that effort we deserved something special. For her, that meant "little rewards". Grandpa didn't much care what the dessert was–as long as it was chocolate. He adored chocolate–chocolate with red wine! Only now are wine lovers discovering the pure joy of this flavor combination, but grandpa knew it fifty years ago.

So whatever your choice, plain or fancy, give your self a "little reward" today.

Apricot Wine Mold

Notes from Patti:

This is a wonderful dessert for dinner parties since it can be made the day before. I don't like serving too rich or heavy desserts if there has been four or more courses.

1 Tbsp. unflavored gelatin
1/4 cup cold water
1 cup heavy cream
1 cup powdered sugar
1/2 cup fresh squeezed lemon juice
2 Tbsp. fresh grated lemon peel
1/2 cup apricot wine
10-12 fresh apricots, seeded and cut in fourths
1/4 cup slivered toasted almonds

Soften gelatin in cold water and set aside. Beat cream until it holds soft peaks. Add sugar and beat until thoroughly mixed. Fold in lemon juice and lemon peel. Heat the apricot wine just to boiling and add softened gelatin. Cool to room temperature Gradually add to cream mixture and blend thoroughly. Pour into a 9" ring mold and chill until firm. Unmold on platter. Fill the center with apricots and garnish with toasted almonds. Serves 6. No substitute for apricot wine.

Almond Stuffed Apricots

I love anything apricotty and these little tidbits are a delightful and satisfying snack.

1–8 oz. almond paste, cut in small pieces
1 Tbsp. almond marsala
48 jumbo dried apricots
1/2 cup coarse baking sugar

In a small bowl, cream almond paste and almond marsala until smooth. Place a level teaspoon mixture onto the middle of each apricot. Bring up sides of apricots, squeezing gently to almost cover filling. Roll in sugar to coat. Place on rack in a cool spot and dry overnight. Store in airtight container. Will store up to 2 weeks. Makes 48. Any almond flavored liqueur may be substituted for the almond marsala.

Grandma's Steamed Persimmon Pudding

This recipe is very special to me because it brings back wonderful childhood memories. In late October we began to watch the persimmons turn color and I would pester Mama everyday as to when she would make the pudding. It was almost like waiting for Christmas morning-the anticipation was overwhelming-finally she would decide the persimmons were just right and I would be allowed to pick the fruit. To this day I think of Mama when I see a persimmon tree.

1/3 cup butter, softened
1 cup brown sugar
2 eggs, beaten
2 1/2 cups all-purpose flour
1/4 tsp. salt
2 1/2 tsps. baking powder
1/2 tsp. cinnamon
1/4 tsp. nutmeg
1/3 cup evaporated milk
1 cup persimmon pulp

Butter a two quart mold and set aside. Cream the butter in a bowl and slowly add the sugar. Stir in the eggs. Mix flour, salt, baking powder, cinnamon and nutmeg together and add with the milk, to the butter mixture. Beat until well blended. Add persimmon pulp and blend until pulp is completely incorporated. Pour batter into mold and cover tightly. Choose a large pot with a cover in which the mold will fit when the pot is covered. Set a rack in the pot to raise the mold so that water can circulate all around it. Place mold on rack and add enough boiling water to the pot so the mold will be covered halfway up it's sides. Cover and steam for 2 1/2 hours. Remove and let cool for 20 minutes before unmolding. Serve plain or with whipped cream or hard sauce. Serves 8 generously.

Olallieberry Cobbler

"Olallie" is the name given to blackberries by the Indians of the lower Columbia River Valley. In appearance, they are rather long and cone shaped and a little darker in color. This is the first dessert my family asks for when berries are in season.

Notes from Patti:

This is fun to make. As the cobbler bakes, the crust rises to the top.

1 1/2 cups prepared biscuit mix
2 Tbsps. sugar
1/2 cup milk
1 pint fresh olallieberries, hulled and rinsed
1/2 cup sugar
1 cup olallieberry wine
3 Tbsps. butter
1/4 tsps. powdered cinnamon

Mix biscuit mix with 2 tablespoons sugar, add milk and stir until well blended. Butter a 2 quart casserole and spread batter over the bottom. Add olallieberries and sprinkle with 1/2 cup sugar and cinnamon. In a small saucepan, heat olallieberry wine and butter to the boiling point and pour over fresh olallieberries. Bake in a preheated 375°F oven for 45 minutes. Serves 6. There is no substitute for olallieberry wine.

Raspberry Poached Pears

This is one of my favorite winter desserts. A real relief from the overly rich fruit cakes and holiday puddings. The pears can be poached with any medium dry or sweet wine, but I especially like the delicate flavor that the Raspberry wine lends to this dish.

3 cups raspberry wine
1 cup water
1 1/2 cups sugar
1 whole orange peel, cut in julienne strips
4 cloves
6 large fresh pears, with stems

Place raspberry wine, water, sugar, orange strips, and cloves in a pan large enough to hold the pears. Bring to a simmer and cook, stirring constantly until sugar is dissolved. Raise the heat and boil 8 to 10 minutes. While syrup cooks, peel pears, being careful to leave the stems on. Slice small bit off each bottom so that the pears can stand upright securely. Add pears to syrup and poach 10 to 15 minutes until tender but firm. Arrange on dessert plates, pour equal amounts of syrup over each serving. Garnish with sprigs of mint. Serves 6.

Wine Frosted Grapes

This is an elegant dessert to end a festive meal where many courses have been served. Just the right bit of sweetness for the palate.

1 lb. white seedless grapes
1 lb. red seedless grapes
1–750 ml Sweet Gewurztraminer
1 Tbsp. grated lemon zest
Granulated sugar

Cut grapes into small clusters. Mix Sweet Gewurztraminer with lemon zest in a large bowl. Add grapes and cover. Refrigerate 24 hours. Line cookie sheet with waxed paper. Remove grapes from marinade and place on cookie sheet. Sprinkle with sugar. Place in freezer for 1 hour before serving. Serves 6. Sweet Johannisberg Riesling may be substituted for Gewurztraminer.

Dressed Up Honeydew Melon

Honeydew melons are one of my favorite melons and while I like it plain, it even more of a treat all dressed up!

1 large honeydew melon
3 pints fresh strawberries, stemmed
2 cups White Zinfandel

Cut out a lid about 4 inches in diameter around the stem end of the melon, making a zig-zag edge. Scrape the seeds off the lid and set aside. Spoon out and discard the seeds from the cavity of melon. With a melon baller, scoop out the flesh, being careful not to pierce the skin. Stem strawberries and cut in half lengthwise. Mix strawberries with melon balls and White Zinfandel. Return to honeydew shell, cover with lid and refrigerate for several hours. Serve the fruit directly from the melon shell. Serves 6. No substitutes for White Zinfandel.

Strawberries and Ricotta Cream

This is a family favorite and a snap to make.

1 pint plus 6 strawberries
1 Tbsp. superfine sugar
1–15 oz. container ricotta cheese
1/2 cup confectioners' sugar, sifted
1 tsp. orange marsala
1 Tbsp. grated orange peel

Wash and hull strawberries. Set aside 6 of the prettiest berries and slice the rest. In a medium bowl, toss the berries with sugar and refrigerate. Whip the cheese in a medium mixing bowl with mixer at high speed. Beat in confectioners' sugar and orange marsala until mixture is smooth and light. Stir in orange peel. Divide sliced berries between 6 wide mouth champagne glasses. Top each serving with ricotta cream and garnish with a whole strawberry. Chill. Serves 6. You may substitute any orange flavored liqueur for the orange marsala.

Notes from Patti:

This dessert is such fun to make because you can use any fresh fruit or toppings you like. Try tangerine slices topped with grated semi-sweet chocolate.

Liqueured Strawberries

2 pints strawberries, stemmed and rinsed
1/3 cup sugar
1/3 cup orange flavored marsala
1 orange

Pat strawberries dry with paper toweling and put in a bowl. Sprinkle with sugar and the orange marsala. Using a potato peeler, cut around the orange to produce a thin spiral of peel. Be careful not to cut into the white pulp. Cut into thin shreds and add to strawberries. Gently fold to cover the berries with all ingredients. Cover the bowl with plastic wrap and refrigerate 3 to 6 hours. Serves 6. Grand Marnier may be substituted for orange Marsala.

Riesling Soft Custard

Notes from Patti:

Unlike most varietal wines, Johannisberg Riesling varies a great deal in style. Some are quite dry while others are very sweet. The sweeter styles are usually labeled "Late Harvest", or even "botrytis cinerea", known as the noble mold. The resultant wine has lucious fruit aromas, reminiscent of citrus, spice, apricot and honey, which add greatly to the taste of this soft custard.

This recipe is the best example I can think of in favor of the argument for the use of the very best wine in food.

3 large egg yolks
6 Tbsps. superfine sugar
1/2 cup sweet Johannisberg Riesling
1/4 tsp. grated lemon peel
1 tsp. orange marsala

Whisk egg yolks and sugar briskly until sugar is dissolved, in the insert of a double boiler. Set insert over, but not touching, simmering water and cook, whisking constantly, until eggs begin to thicken, 3 to 4 minutes. Gradually add Johannisberg Riesling and continue to cook, whisking constantly, until mixture is thickened and tripled in volume, about 8 more minutes. Whisk in lemon and orange marsala. Pour into champagne glasses. Garnish with orange slices and serve at once. Serves 4. There is no substitute for Johannisberg Riesling. Any orange liqueur, such as Kirsch, may be substituted for orange marsala.

Raspberry Chocolate Mousse

This combination of flavors is wonderfully pleasing to the palate.
I serve small glasses of raspberry wine with the mousse.

8 oz. semi-sweet chocolate
1 tsp. vanilla
2 large eggs plus 2 egg yolks
1/4 cup sugar
1/2 pint heavy cream
3 Tbsps. raspberry wine

Raspberry Sauce

1 package frozen raspberries
3 Tbsps. sugar

Break chocolate into small pieces and melt in a double boiler, over
hot water. While chocolate melts, add eggs, yolks, vanilla and sugar
to food processor fitted with a steel blade and blend. Add the cream
and raspberry wine and blend. With motor running pour melted
chocolate through feed tube. Scrape down sides of work bowl once or
twice if needed. Divide between 8 cream pots or champagne glasses
cover with plastic wrap and refrigerate until firm–about an hour.
Process raspberries with sugar in food processor fitted with steel
blade until smooth. Refrigerate. Spoon over chocolate mousse just
before serving. Raspberry liqueur may be substituted for raspberry
wine. Serves 8 chocoholics.

Grandma's Orange Fudge Cupcakes

I've already mentioned my Grandfather's great fondness for chocolate. If asked what he would like for dessert, his reply was always the same—"I don't care as long as it's chocolate". These cupcakes were his favorite.

Notes from Patti:

Citrus peel freezes very well. When I need orange or lemon peel, I will peel the whole orange or lemon, dice it and freeze for future use.

1 lb. butter (must be butter)
8 oz. sweet baking chocolate, broken into small pieces
3 1/2 cups sugar
2 cups all-purpose flour
1/8 tsp. salt
8 eggs, room temperature
1 tsp. vanilla
1 Tbsp. orange marsala
1 Tbsp. finely diced orange peel
4 cups coarsely chopped pecans
36 pecan halves

Preheat oven to 300°F. Line muffin pans with paper cups. Melt butter and chocolate in top of a double boiler. Set over simmering water. Combine sugar, flour and salt in a large bowl. Stir in chocolate mixture. Add eggs, vanilla, orange marsala, and orange rind and whisk just until ingredients are evenly moistened; do not overmix. Fold in chopped pecans. Spoon batter into muffin cups, filling 2/3 full. Top each with 1 pecan half and bake 40 minutes or until tester inserted in centers comes out clean. Makes 36. Any orange flavored liqueur may be substituted for orange marsala.

Sonny's Chocolate Mint Kisses

3 large egg whites, room temperature
1 tsp. white wine vinegar
1 cup sugar
3 drops green food coloring
12 oz. mint flavored chocolate chips

Preheat oven to 350°F for 30 minutes. Line 2 baking sheets with a double thickness of waxed paper. Beat egg whites and vinegar in largest bowl of electric mixer until soft peaks form. Add sugar, 1 tablespoon at a time and continue to beat until stiff but not dry. Tint mixture with food coloring until light green. Fold in chocolate chips. Drop mixture by heaping teaspoons onto prepared baking sheets. Place in oven and immediately TURN OFF HEAT. DO NOT OPEN OVEN DOOR for at least 6 hours. Carefully remove from paper and store in an air tight container. Makes 60 to 70 kisses.

Notes from Patti:

I like to make these in the evening and leave them in the oven over night. However, if you have any little (or big) gremlins in your house, you best be the first one up in the morning or you may find your kisses gone!

Brandy Balls

These little cookies always show up during the Christmas holidays but I keep them on hand all year. I always serve them with fresh fruit.

3 cups finely crumbled vanilla wafer cookies
1 cup powdered sugar, sifted
2 Tbsps. cocoa
3 Tbsps. corn syrup
1 cup finely chopped pecans
1/2 cup flaked coconut
1/3 cup brandy

In a large bowl, combine all ingredients and mix well. Using a tablespoon, scoop up a spoonful of the mixture. Put the spoonful into the palm of your hand and use the other palm to roll the mixture into a 1" ball. Store in a covered container for 2 to 3 days to allow the flavors to "marry". Yields 40 balls.

Double Chocolate Chip Cheesecake

Notes from Patti:

You can refrigerate this cake up to five days–not that it will last that long! It is also a wonderful do ahead since it freezes very well.

1 1/2 cups chocolate wafer crumbs (about 25 wafers)
3/4 stick butter, room temperature
1/3 cup sugar
2–8 oz. packages cream cheese, room temperature
1 1/4 cups sugar, divided
4 eggs
1 tsp. vanilla
1 1/2 cups sour cream, divided
1–6 oz. package semisweet chocolate chips
1 1/2 tsps. orange marsala
1 1/2 tsps. lemon juice

Position rack in center of oven and preheat to 325°F. Butter bottom and sides of 9 inch springform pan. Combine crumbs, butter and sugar in medium bowl and mix well. Pat evenly onto bottom and sides of prepared pan. Chill. In large bowl beat cream cheese and 3/4 cup sugar until smooth. Beat in eggs and 1 teaspoon vanilla until well blended. Stir in 1/2 cup sour cream and chocolate chips until well blended. Pour into crust. Bake in preheated 325°F oven 40 minutes or until 3 inch circle in center jiggles when pan is moved gently. (Cheesecake becomes firm when cooled). Removed from oven; cool in pan on rack 20 minutes. Increase oven temperature to 425°F. Mix well remaining 1 cup sour cream, remaining 1/2 cup sugar, 1 1/2 teaspoons orange marsala and 1 1/2 teaspoons lemon juice. Spoon evenly over top of cheesecake. Return to oven; bake 5 minutes longer. Cool completely and chill. To serve, remove sides of pan and let stand 1 hour at room temperature. Serves 10 easily.

Pumpkin Cheesecake

20 gingersnaps
1 cup walnuts
3 Tbsps. butter, melted

1–8oz. package cream cheese
1/4 cup sugar
1/2 tsp. vanilla

1 egg
1–16 oz. can pumpkin
2/3 cup evaporated milk
2 eggs
1/2 cup sugar
2 Tbsps. walnut marsala
1 tsp. cinnamon
1/4 tsp. nutmeg
1/4 tsp. ginger

Notes from Patti:

I have spent Thanksgiving with my dear friends Joan and Garry Deuel for years. I always bring wine and dessert. One year Joanie asked me to make cheesecake. Somehow a plain cheesecake didn't seem festive enough for the holiday. I found gingersnaps, pumpkin and walnuts in my cabinets and a picture began to dance in my head. I knew the flavors would come together and I thought it would look great—I was right on both counts. It's easy to prepare, but always looks as if it came from a fancy bakery.

Place gingersnaps in food processor fitted with steel blade and process until gingersnaps are coarse crumbs. Pour into mixing bowl. Add walnuts to processor and process until nuts are coarsely chopped. Add to gingersnaps. Add butter and mix well. Press mixture onto bottom of a 9 inch spring form pan. Combine softened cream cheese, sugar and vanilla, mixing until well blended. Blend in egg and mix until mixture is fluffy. Spoon over crumb mixture. Combine remaining ingredients and carefully spoon over cheese mixture. Bake in a preheated 325°F degree oven 1 1/2 hours or until set. Loosen cake from rim of pan. Cool to room temperature. Chill several hours before serving. Serves 10 to 12.

John's Heart Attack Cake

John Smith, owner/chef of the Salmon Poacher Restaurant in Soquel, California, is a truly gifted chef. His approach to food is traditional yet he is always innovative. He uses only fresh ingredients and has a superb sense of seasonings. The restaurant is cozy without being fussy and the beautiful roses on the tables are grown by John.

Notes from Patti:

If you are a chocoholic, this cake is for you! It is not at all difficult to make. It does take some time but not much more than any cake made from scratch. This cake is a real show stopper and the appreciation you will receive is well worth your time. John serves the cake with vanilla sauce streaked with strained pureed raspberries. The easiest vanilla sauce is a good vanilla ice cream, melted at room temperature.

20 oz. chocolate (the best you can get)
1 1/4 cups superfine sugar
1 lb. unsalted butter
1/4 cup Grand Marnier
10 egg yolks
10 egg whites
1/4 cup superfine sugar

Melt chocolate in top of double boiler over very low heat. When chocolate has melted, whisk in sugar, mixing well until sugar has dissolved. Whisk in butter and melt, stirring often. When butter is completely incorporated, remove from fire and whisk in Grand Marnier. Whip egg yolks until light and fluffy. Slowly add chocolate mixture to egg yolks whipping constantly until fully incorporated. Return chocolate mixture to mixing bowl and set aside. Whip egg whites until foamy and add remaining sugar and continue whipping until stiff. Place egg whites in bowl with chocolate and fold together. When mixture is smooth and all lumps are gone, pour into buttered and floured 12" spring form pan. Bake at 275°F for three hours. Remove from oven, let rest 20 minutes. Invert onto plate and remove form. Dust with powdered sugar and serve with vanilla sauce and/or raspberry puree.

Chocolate Torte with Butter Cream

My grandfather was a real chocoholic. As a child, I would save my pennies so I could buy him a big 5 pound chocolate bar for his birthday. He would hide it away and, as generous a man as he was, would not share that chocolate with anyone. I must have been about 16 when I made a chocolate torte for him. From that day forward, he always let me know he wanted the torte for his birthday.

1/4 cup fine bread crumbs
5 oz. almonds
4 oz. semi-sweet chocolate, cut in small pieces
1/4 lb. butter (must be butter)
2/3 cup sugar
3 large eggs
2 Tbsps. orange marsala
Grated rind of one orange

Notes from Patti:

When using a double boiler for any food, the insert pan should never touch the water in the lower pan. This is most important to remember when you are dealing with chocolate. If the water is too hot, the chocolate will become gritty. Most chocolate chips are not meant to be melted, they are designed for cookies.

Preheat oven to 375°F. Butter an 8" cake pan and line the bottom of the pan with buttered paper. Dust with 2 tablespoons of the bread crumbs and set aside. Place almonds in the bowl of a food processor fitted with a steel blade and process until almonds are very fine. Set aside. Melt chocolate in the top of a double boiler over hot water. With the steel blade still in place, put butter and sugar in the processor bowl and process until fluffy. Add eggs, one at a time, and process quickly. Add chocolate, orange marsala, grated orange rind and remaining bread crumbs. Process just until ingredients are blended. Pour into prepared pan and bake for 25-30 minutes. Cake should be soft and moist. Don't worry if cake is cracked on top. Cool in pan 45 minutes. Unmold and refrigerate for one hour before frosting with butter cream.

Butter Cream

6 oz. semi-sweet chocolate, cut into small pieces
1/4 cup hot, strong coffee
2 Tbsps. powdered sugar
4 egg yolks
1/2 cup butter
2 Tbsps. orange marsala

Melt chocolate in top of double boiler over hot water. Place melted chocolate in processor bowl fitted with a steel blade. Add all other ingredients and process until smooth. Chill to spreadable consistency and frost torte.

Raspberry Wine Tarts

These little tarts are wonderfully delicate but the problem is you can't eat just one! Plan on a least three per guest and serve a small glass of the raspberry wine with them. Perfect for a dinner party when a rich dessert is inappropriate.

1 1/2 cups all-purpose flour
2/3 cup butter
7 tsps. raspberry wine
8 oz. raspberry jam
1 cup granulated sugar

Sift flour and work in butter with a pastry cutter until dough is crumbly. Add raspberry wine a little at a time until dough has the consistency of pastry dough. Roll out on a floured board and cut with a 3" diameter biscuit cutter or wine glass. Place 1/2 teaspoon raspberry jam in center and fold over in half, crimping edges with a fork. Bake in a 350°F for 13 to 14 minutes. Remove from oven and roll in sugar. Yields about 3 dozen. No substitute for raspberry wine.

Hot Spiced Honey Wine

1 750 ml. honey wine
1/2" cinnamon stick
2 whole cloves
2 whole allspice

6 to 8 hours before serving open wine and add spices. Recork and let stand at room temperature until ready to heat. Pour into crock pot and heat just until bubbles appear around the edges. Serve at once in heated mugs. A double boiler may be used if you don't have a crock pot.

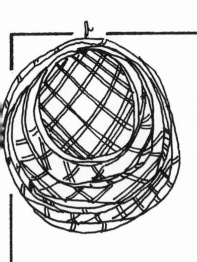

Additional Notes from Patti

This is not meant to be a glossary--only notes that reflect some of my thoughts. I know I have strong (some have even said opinionated) feelings about food and wine, be that as it may, I hope you glean a little here and a bit there that you find useful or makes you happy or gives you a smidgen of pleasure from their reading.

As I finish this work my mind is reeling with all the thoughts, I haven't shared with you. Perhaps we will meet again in yet another book.

Basil

Someday I'm going to write a book about basil and all it's delights. Those who know me will tell you I eat pesto on toast! It is the perfect herb for any food containing tomatoes. Try it sprinkled over baked potatoes with a bit of sour cream, and those tiny leaves liven up any green salad. I have been known to drive for miles to find a farmer who grows basil and buy it by the bushel–no little bunches for me–for making pesto, which I freeze in ice cube trays and store for winter because I can't last from season to season without pesto. I also freeze leaves in thin layers of oil for other uses. The next time you see a bunch of fresh basil, take it home and liven up your taste buds.

Pine Nuts (Pignolia)

Pine nuts are probably the least known nut in the United States, but in other parts of the world, notably Northern Italy, they often replace meat in the diet. They are tiny kernels of certain pine cones and are quite oily with a delicate flavor, and are best toasted 10 to 15 minutes before using. One of the simplest, but most elegant sauces for pasta, is

pine nuts browned in garlic flavored olive oil with a handful of fresh basil tossed in at the last second. Pour this over fresh pasta and you have a wonderful meal. Take the time to find a shop or health food store that features a wide variety of nuts and buy in bulk–they are much cheaper and freeze very well.

Garlic

For me it is <u>always</u> necessary to use fresh garlic. It should be plump and firm with paperlike covering, never spongy or shriveled. Garlic should be stored in a cool dry place that has good ventilation. If garlic is kept too long, or it sprouts, it will loose much of its pungency and flavor. Buy smaller amounts and replace as needed. Should you live in an area (the moon?) where fresh garlic is unavailable year round, or should you be lucky enough to be given a large supply, peel the garlic and drop into pint jars and cover with a good olive oil. Not only will the oil preserve the garlic for several months but provide you with instant garlic flavored oil for cooking.

Parsley

There are two kinds of parsley. The bright green curly parsley, used all too often as a garnish and the wide leaf, dark green Italian parsley that gives intense flavor. Italian parsley is not widely available commercially because once picked it tends to wilt easily. My personal favorite is the Italian parsley. Fortunately it grows nicely in window pots. Whatever you choice, both add great flavor and color to food. Should you be adverse to the smell of garlic, munch a little parsley–it's loaded with chlorophyll.

Mustard

As a child, we didn't have jars of mustard in the refrigerator to slap haphazardly on just any food. Grandma made her mustards to accompany what she was serving. They were never the same because she used no recipe, only her taste buds. They ranged from hot to sweet with every conceivable taste in between. For some she used white wine to achieve a certain flavor she wanted. In others she used sherry for a more distinctive nutty taste. When she made hot mustard, with tiny flecks of devil red peppers in it, you knew it was hot! She used a wide range of herbs, either alone or in combination. There were garlic and lemon flavors for pork and sweet mustard, that made cold chicken a treat. When Grandma made mustard she used a mortar and pestle. Today, with the use of a food processor, you can have instant mustard with any flavor that sits your fancy. I have just noticed a bowl of lemons on the table and there is fresh dill in my kitchen window box...excuse me, I have to make some mustard for dinner.

Mushrooms

I have opted to use only commercially grown mushrooms (agaricus) in this work because I am committed to using readily available foods. I have fastidiously avoided wild mushrooms, not because I don't like them, but because one has to be absolutely positive about what they are picking. The wrong species can make you very ill and some can kill you.

At this writing, dried, imported mushrooms are very much in vogue. These are quite good but they do require the user to have some knowledge of them since they are usually quite intense in taste and can detract rather than add flavor to a dish if improper used. With these thoughts in mind, I leave it up to your preferences and use of this ancient and magical food.

Vinegar

The array of vinegars on the market today is mind boggling. Time was you didn't think much about vinegar–you bought distilled vinegar for pickling and fermented vinegar for cooking. Today there are vinegars infused with every herb you ever heard of, and the list of fruit vinegars is growing daily. There are blackberry, raspberry, strawberry and whatever berry–there's peach, pear, apricot and of course the citrus

varieties. This is all well and good as long as you don't end up, as a friend of mine did, with 10 or 12 bottles of vinegar that were not in her normal usage. For general cooking, I still find good wine vinegar the most adaptable for me. There is also great variety in these vinegars. Aside from red and white wine vinegars, there are those made for sherry and sparkling wine and I recently received a vinegar made from Zinfandel grapes. I will not offer advice about your choices but remind you that the old saying "a spendthrift for oil, a miser for vinegar" is still excellent advice.

Olive Oil

I don't just like olive oil, I'm crazy about it and almost never use any other kind of oil. I have used olive oil from every part of the world that the tree grows and simply put, my friend, Nick Sciabica and his family make the best olive oil I've ever tasted. They have been in business for over 50 years and the standards they have established for their unrefined 100% virgin olive fruit oils far exceed the quality requirements for imported olive oils. They use only premium tree fruit and they process the olives one time, producing only the first flow of oil from the fruit. No reprocessing is ever done for higher yields of inferior oil, and the olive oil is never refined. Mr. Sciabica will tell you their oils are 100% pure virgin, as they are in nature. Nick takes as much care and has as much pride in his fine oils as any wine maker takes with his fine wine. You can find cheaper priced oils than Nick Sciabica's but you will never find a better quality or more flavorful oil than his.

Italians and Greeks-the largest consumers of olive oil have long known the health benefits of the olive. Recent medical studies show these people have low levels of plasma cholesterol and a low rate of heart disease. There is a wonderful new book titled the Mediterranean Diet by Carol and Malcolm McConnell, (which I hasten to add has nothing to do with those tacky weight loss books)–is a serious work on the value of wine, pasta and olive oil in our diets. Its great to know that something that tastes so good can be so good for us.

Lemons

This brilliant yellow citrus fruit always makes me smile. There is something about its color and smell that simply makes me feel good. It is inexpensive, always available and, as far as I am concerned, an irreplaceable ingredient in cooking. There is no comparison between fresh lemon juices and flavorings. We use them in everything from soup to desserts. I cannot imagine fish without lemon and if you have never eaten lemon chicken, you haven't lived. I can never let a year go by without at least one great big fat lemon meringue pie. Grandma always kept a lemon or two in her linen closet and everything in there smelled wonderful. How better to greet an old friend on a sweltering summer day than the offer or ice cold, homemade lemonade–none I can think of.

Chocolate

As we grow older, hopefully, we grown in experience and knowledge. One of those growth areas in my culinary life has been chocolate. I came to the glaring realization that my knowledge was more in my mouth than my brain. During the last few years, I've been fortunate to meet some lovely people in the chocolate business. Among that elite group, Phyllis Larsen of Ghiradelli Chocolate. She has been most generous with both her time and knowledge and gave me both with much good humor. The experts all agree on some basic steps. First, buy the very best chocolate you can find. Second, read the label, there is a lot of artificial chocolate on the market. Some chocolate, like chips and morsels, can contain paraffin to prevent melting so the pieces retain their shapes. Third, and the most important step, is the way chocolate is melted. Start by breaking the chocolate into small pieces. A food processor fitted with a steel blade is ideal for this job. Put the chocolate in the top of a double boiler–being careful the insert pan never touches the water. Use hot, but never boiling water. Never cover the pot with a lid. This will cause condensation and drops of water will fall into the chocolate causing it to "tighten" or stiffen and become unworkable. If this happens, quickly whisk in 1 to 2 tablespoons of vegetable shortening to re-liquify.

Today we are inundated with books, magazines and food columns devoted entirely to chocolate. I don't know about you but I never tire of reading, experimenting and eating this lovely stuff–and I promise never again to recommend chocolaty chips unless they are in cookies.

Wine

After all these years, I am still spellbound by the magic of wine and what it does for food. My aim is to give you some guidelines in your culinary efforts. It is often said there is no right or wrong way with wine, and I agree with that point of view. I firmly believe your own taste is your best guide.

For the purpose of this book, I have used no generic wine. That is those wines named for geographical locations, such as Chablis and Burgundy, and made from no particular grape varietal. These wines vary widely in flavor and are usually made from lesser quality grapes. This does not mean every wine labeled Chablis or Burgundy is a bad wine. You may find some wine using those names that are flavorful and very appealing to your palate and that is all that matters.

I have already discussed varietal wine in the introduction of this work and stand by those opinions. You will find at the end of each recipe a substitute wine that has worked well for me. In some instances there is no workable substitute

If I could give you a gift it would be the knowledge that even the plainest food can be presented with style and grace and given the air of celebration when it is cooked and served with fine wine.

Fortified Wines

Fortified wines are wines that have added spirits and range from 18% to 21% alcohol by volume. They are drunk as aperitif wines, that is before the meal and dessert wines, served most often with cheese and nuts. These wines, unfortunately, are not in great favor with Americans.

Before Prohibition, many fine fortified wines were produced in this country. When Prohibition was repealed in 1933, the wine market was flooded with cheap, quickly made, high alcohol wines to satisfy the demands of thirsty Americans. Over the next 25 years of or, to the everlasting embarrassment of the wine industry, these cheap wines were bottled in gallon jugs and earned the reputation of "wino" or even worse, cooking wines, as in "cooking sherry". Today there are many fine fortified wines to be found in the market place and they are regaining more and more acceptance.

Fine fortified wines lend themselves especially well to cooking, adding richness of flavor in certain dishes that table wines are unable to give. An additional plus is their staying power. Once opened they last for many months. While it is unnecessary to refrigerate, it is important to store them in a cool cabinet, never above or next to a kitchen stove, sink or any place exposed to sun. They should be looked at as any other food staples-always handy! I keep dry and sweet sherry, dry and sweet vermouth, dry and sweet Marsala, Madeiras and port. I must, once again, emphasize the importance of quality. I do not infer that 25 year old port must be used, but rather a port that is tasty enough to drink.

Index